George
B·U·S·H

George
B·U·S·H

GEORGE SULLIVAN

JULIAN MESSNER

JULIAN MESSNER and colophon are trademarks of
Simon & Schuster, Inc. Design by Meredith Dunham.
Manufactured in the United States of America

Lib. ed. 10 9 8 7 6 5 4 3 2 1

Paper ed. 10 9 8 7 6 5 4 3 2 1

Library of Congress Cataloging-in-Publication Data

Sullivan, George, 1927-
George Bush / George Sullivan.
p. cm.
Bibliography: p. 165
Includes index.
Summary: Examines the life, career, and personal characteristics
of the man who served as vice president for eight years under Ronald
Reagan and was then elected to follow him as the nation's
forty- first president.
1. Bush, George, 1924- —Juvenile literature. 2. Presidents—
United States—Biography—Juvenile literature. 3. United States—
Politics and government—1981-1989—Juvenile literature.
4. Presidents—United States—Election—1988—Juvenile literature.
[1. Bush, George, 1924. 2. Presidents.] I. Title.
E882.S85 1989
973.928'092—dc20
[B]
[92]   89-8349
                                                              CIP
                                                               AC
ISBN 0-671-64599-4   ISBN 0-671-67814-0 (pbk.)

CONTENTS

CHAPTER ONE

A NEW BREEZE

For some Presidents the office was an awesome burden. Thomas Jefferson termed the presidency a "splendid misery." John Quincy Adams called the time he spent in office "the four most miserable years of my life." His successor, Andrew Jackson, called it "a situation of dignified slavery."

But there was none of this hand-wringing for George Bush. When he took over as the nation's forty-first President in January 1989, Bush was serene about public duty. "He intends to enjoy this in the manner of Teddy Roosevelt, not treat it as some dreary drudgery," said C. Boyden Gray, one of Bush's closest advisers.

President Bush believes in government, believes he is capable of making it work. He has described himself as

George Bush flashes a victory smile following his election win in 1988.
(The White House)

1

a man who has "done the work of democracy, day by day."

In August 1988 Bush told the Republican National Convention, "I am a practical man, I like what's real. I'm not much for the airy and abstract, I like what works."

And this was a theme Bush repeated in his inauguration speech in January 1989, promising he would "use power to help people."

"A new breeze is blowing," Bush declared in that speech, "and a nation refreshed by freedom stands ready to push on. There's new ground to be broken and new action to be taken."

George Bush entered the White House as America was enjoying a period of peace and prosperity. There were no crises to be confronted, either domestic or foreign. Relations between the United States and the Soviet Union were more hopeful than at any time in forty years. Polls showed that Americans were pretty much satisfied with the country's direction.

At the same time, Bush inherited a long list of long-postponed national problems. Under Ronald Reagan, who had preceded Bush in office, the nation failed to pay its bills. Government debt, amassed by spending money obtained by borrowing, had skyrocketed.

Reagan had favored smaller government, lower taxes, and increased military spending—and not much else. He was accused of being indifferent to the needs of the disadvantaged, including poor people and blacks.

Bush laid plans to correct such oversights. In the case of social policy, Bush suggested a "kinder, gentler" government that would pay more attention to child care and

After his election win in 1988, Bush met with Rev. Jesse Jackson as well as other political opponents. (Wide World)

President Bush waves to crowd following oath-taking ceremonies at 1989 inaugural.
(George Sullivan)

education. He said he wanted to become known as the "education President."

Bush also would provide more money to aid the millions of homeless people who populated the nation's inner cities.

Bush said he would do more for the environment. He promised to make the nation's beaches free of hypodermic needles. He recognized the peril of acid rain—the rain, snow, and fog polluted by smoke and fumes given off by factories and cars. Acid rain was attacking the environment.

In his inaugural address Bush delivered an unqualified promise to put an end to the epidemic of drug abuse: "Take my word, this scourge will stop."

As he sought solutions for those problems, Bush still exhibited many of the traits he acquired from his parents and family life. He and his wife, Barbara, both children of privilege, are devoted to the idea that the wealthy have an obligation to give something back to society.

This idea gave rise to the term "a thousand points of light," which Bush introduced at the Republican National Convention in August 1988. The term refers to volunteerism, to the voluntary contributions Bush said Americans must make. He expanded the idea in his inaugural address, declaring the country must "turn to the only resource we have that in time of need always grows: the goodness and the courage of the American people."

Bush looks upon public service as an honor and a duty. This idea he attributes to Prescott Bush, who was his tall, stern, and strict father, a self-made millionaire who served for ten years in the United States Senate.

"Dad taught me about duty and service," Bush has said. At the same time, his mother, Dorothy Walker Bush, the daughter of a Wall Street investment banker, taught him not to brag, not to take credit if he could give it to someone else.

Bush was sent to Phillips Academy in Andover, Massachusetts, one of the leading prep schools in the nation. World War II started not long before he graduated, and Bush enlisted in the navy. He later became the navy's youngest pilot. On a bombing run against a Japanese radio transmitter on the island of Chichi Jima, Bush's plane was shot down. Bush bailed out and was rescued, but two crewmen were killed. Their deaths have always weighed heavily on Bush.

After Bush married Barbara Pierce and following his graduation from Yale in 1948, the couple headed for Midland, Texas, to make their own fortune in the oil business. They later moved to Houston. It was there Bush entered politics. After four years in Congress and a defeat for a Senate seat in 1970, Bush was named United Nations ambassador and later chairman of the Republican National Committee.

After Richard Nixon resigned as President in the wake of the Watergate scandal, Gerald Ford, Nixon's successor, named Bush United States envoy to China. He stayed in the post for a year before being called back to head the Central Intelligence Agency.

Bush made his first attempt to win the Republican party's presidential nomination in 1980, pitting himself against Ronald Reagan. After Reagan's victory, Bush was tapped as his running mate.

In the eight years he served as Reagan's Vice President, Bush was always devoted and loyal. "When the administration jumped," said Richard Williamson, a Reagan aide, "Bush jumped too."

Once a political moderate, Bush often seemed to be a Reagan conservative. "He submerged his own views," said former Maryland Senator Charles Mathias.

The strategy worked. Bush managed to escape being closely tied to many of the shortcomings of the Reagan administration. With the help of his longtime friend Jim Baker, he began laying the groundwork for the 1988 race.

He rose to the challenges as they presented themselves. He shook off a defeat in Iowa early in the campaign, bouncing back with a win in the New Hampshire primary. He rebounded again in the fall of 1988 against his Democratic opponent, Massachusetts Governor Michael Dukakis.

Not long before his inauguration, Bush said in an interview with Walter Mears of the Associated Press that he was not planning any dramatic changes in the opening months of his administration. "I've been part of this administration," he said, "and it isn't like there is need for radical change. People understood that when they voted," Bush added. "They weren't looking for a radical shift."

Bush, however, continued to emphasize that he would pay more attention to some of the social problems that were low on the Reagan administration's list of priorities. In his budget message to Congress early in 1989, Bush stressed he was seeking to promote education, reduce

Bush shakes hands with enthusiastic school children on visit to Philadelphia during 1988 campaign for the presidency.
(The White House)

homelessness, curb illegal narcotics, and help the poor.

No one could say for sure how Bush intended to achieve his goals. The big question: How could Bush fully fund the programs he outlined?

"The overriding definition of '89 is going to be, 'There ain't no money,'" said Stephen Hess of the Brookings Institution.

Bush could not raise taxes. His solemn vow during the campaign was that he would not.

But without a tax increase, where would the money come from to pay for the programs Bush had proposed?

At the time he became President, George Bush had spent a quarter of a century in government. With his knowledge and experience, with his nuts-and-bolts approach, he sincerely believed he could make government work.

But how did he intend to keep taxes low and get the government to do more? Providing an answer to that question was George Bush's first major test as President. Without an answer, the new breeze would not blow for very long.

CHAPTER TWO

VITAL STATISTICS

H ere are some things to know about George Herbert Walker Bush:

• His favorite television program is "NFL Monday Night Football."

• He's allergic to bee stings.

• As Vice President, he kept an Oak Ridge Boys tape in his briefcase to play on the cassette deck in his limousine.

• He can't dance well.

• His favorite movie stars are Clark Gable and Jimmy Stewart.

• He is left-handed (the fourth left-handed President).

• His favorite magazine is the fishing journal *Bassmaster*, and he is a subscriber to *Horseshoe News Digest*.

George Bush is six feet, two inches tall, 195 pounds. He has brown hair and blue eyes. He keeps trim by jogging several times a week and playing tennis. Like Presidents Ford and Carter, he makes frequent use of the White House tennis courts. He also enjoys pitching horseshoes, fishing, and boating.

During the years he served as Vice President, and even before, Bush, when he traveled, went prepared to play tennis. He played on trips to the People's Republic of China, Pakistan, Australia, and Sweden. Once, on a trip to Chi-

Bush is an avid tennis player. Here he teams with President Gerald Ford on the White House court.
(Gerald R. Ford Library)

na, Bush scored a tennis victory over Wan Li, who, at the time Bush became President in 1989, served as chairman of the congress of the People's Republic.

When Bush plays tennis, the Secret Service first checks out the court and dressing-room facilities. Then, during the match, the agents stand close to the court. It doesn't distract Bush because he's used to it, but his opponents get nervous.

The Bush vacation retreat in Kennebunkport, Maine, offers a splendid all-weather tennis court. There the Bushes used to schedule an annual tournament—the Bush family versus members of the Vice President's Secret Service detail, or, as the sides were called, the "Agent Bashers" versus the "Bush Whackers."

Bush also plays horseshoes, a game for two or four players in which the idea is to toss a U-shaped iron shoe around a short stake that is forty feet away. Bush, who has played the game since childhood, is very skilled at it. He has trounced family members, Cabinet members, Secret Service agents, and media representatives.

Bush loves baseball too. He cheers mostly for the Houston Astros, a team he has watched since the 1960s, when he lived in Texas and was just beginning to get involved in politics.

Bush has a rich background as a baseball player. In 1942, when he was attending preparatory school at Phillips Academy in Andover, Massachusetts, the slick-fielding Bush caught the eye of Clark Griffiths, owner of the Washington Senators. "I'd like to have this boy play for the Senators this summer," Bush has quoted

Also a horseshoe enthusiast, Bush competes against family members, friends, Secret Service agents, staff members —anyone.
(Wide World)

Bush has been a baseball fan for more than forty years. Here he throws out the first pitch at a Little League World Series game.
(The White House)

Today Bush keeps trim and fit by frequent jogging.
(The White House)

Griffiths as saying. "It's wartime and I'm short of players."

Bush never signed a contract with the Senators. Instead he enlisted in the navy. Afterward, at Yale, Bush, a first baseman, played for an outstanding college team, one that came close to winning the National Collegiate Athletic Association title two years in a row.

Bush was called "Poppy" in those days. Captain of the team, he was a left-handed fielder and a right-handed batter. He once described himself as "a good fielder and fair hitter."

Bush once even used a bit of baseball in diplomacy. In 1986, when he was Vice President, he took New York Mets' catcher Gary Carter and Houston Astros' pitcher Nolan Ryan with him to the inauguration of the new president of Honduras.

What are the things that are important to George Bush? His family—his wife and children.

"I couldn't live without her, and she couldn't live without me," Bush has said of his wife Barbara, or "Bar," as she is called by her husband, her family, and close friends.

A year younger than her husband, and well known for her crown of silver-gray hair, Barbara Bush has blue-green eyes, a deep, rich voice, and, the Washington *Times* once pointed out, "enough strength and determination to pull a loaded hay wagon if it were required of her."

Bush has often said that nothing gives him greater pride than the fact that he has five children who lived through the 1960s and still love their mother and father. The children are all married now and with kids of their own. The boys are all successful businessmen. They live their own

Of his wife Barbara, Bush has said, "I couldn't live without her."
(Wide World)

lives in different parts of the United States. Although they manage to maintain their independence, they stay close as a family. Every summer they visit the family vacation home at Kennebunkport, Maine, with their families.

"The most fun I have today in my life," Bush has said, "is when I'm doing something with my grandchildren or with our boys and Doro [daughter Dorothy]. It's the most fun. Nothing else compares, nothing."

There are no bad apples in the Bush family. There have been no headlines concerning alcohol or drug abuse. There have been no broken families. The Bush children agree that their parents set a good example. They can't, for instance, ever remember them fighting.

During the years he was Vice President, Bush often kept in touch with his children by means of handwritten notes on blue-bordered cards. "I've saved them since I was little," Dorothy once told the New York *Daily News*. "He wrote me letters when my children were born. Things like, 'Just want you to know that we can't wait to see our grandchild and welcome him and hold him.'"

Bush disciplined his children without ever raising his voice. His method was simply to say that he was disappointed. "As far as I was concerned," Bush's son Jeb once said, "that was the most brutal form of discipline. He loved us so much and we loved him. And simply by saying he was disappointed had a bigger impact than whacking us with a belt."

The children are:

• George Walker Bush, forty-two, of Washington, D.C.; a graduate of the Yale class of 1968; also holds a graduate degree in Business Administration from Harvard, 1975; an Air Force trained pilot in the Texas Air National Guard; ran for Congress in 1978 and lost; recently merged his oil and gas exploration company into Harken Oil and Gas of Dallas, and remains a director of that firm. He and his wife, Laura, have twin girls, Jenna Welch and Barbara Pierce.

• John Ellis "Jeb" Bush, thirty-five, of Tallahassee, Florida; appointed secretary of the Florida Commerce Department in 1987; chairman of the Dade County Republican Party, 1984 to 1986; awarded a degree in Latin American Studies, University of Texas, 1974; went to León, Mexico, on a transfer program and met his wife, Columba, who still holds her Mexican citizenship. They have three children: George Prescott, Noelle Lucila, and John Ellis.

• Neil Mallon Bush, thirty-three, of Denver, Colorado; experienced geologist; involved in oil exploration and drilling; general partner, JNB Exploration Company; holds B.A. degree in International Relations from Tulane University, 1977, and graduate degree in business, also from Tulane, 1979; served as campaign manager for his brother George's race for Congress; he and his wife Sharon have two children, Lauren Pierce and Pierce Mallon.

• Marvin Pierce Bush, thirty-two, of Alexandria, Virginia; owns and operates investment firm, Marvin Bush Associates, in Washington, D.C.; holds B.A. degree in English from the University of Virginia, 1981; married, with one child, Marshall Lloyd.

• Dorothy "Doro" Walker Bush LeBlond, twenty-nine, of Cape Elizabeth, Maine; holds a B.A. degree in Sociolo-

gy from Boston College, 1980; worked as a travel agent
and in art gallery; treasurer of the Republican Town Committee; her husband, Billy, is in the construction business;
two children, Samuel Bush and Nancy Ellis.

All of the Bush children were involved in the presidential campaign of 1988. Son George recalls a family meeting in which his father introduced his campaign manager,
Lee Atwater.

George raised his hand and asked, "How do we know
we can trust Lee Atwater?" He noted that Atwater's business partner had worked for New York Congressman Jack
Kemp, one of Bush's rivals for the Republican nomination.

Later Bush's son spoke to Atwater. "We expect the ut-
most loyalty because we love this guy," he said, referring
to his dad. We are motivated by love. *You* are motivated
by politics."

Atwater listened attentively. "The minute you feel I'm
being disloyal," said Atwater, "fire me." He suggested that
George move to Washington and keep an eye on him.

George did just that. He moved to Washington and became the family's full-time representative at campaign
headquarters.

The Republican National Convention in New Orleans
was often a family affair for the Bushes. Bush's daughter-
in-law Columba spoke in both English and Spanish as she
seconded the nomination of the man she said "has been
like a father to me."

The most visible family members were Bush's five children, all of whom had been elected delegates from their
home states. George W. Bush, the Vice President's eldest

*The Bush family poses for a group photo near family home
at Kennebunkport, Maine.
(Office of the Vice President)*

son, was a delegate from Texas; Jeb Bush was a Florida delegate; Neil Bush was a Colorado delegate; Marvin Bush was a Virginia delegate; and Dorothy Bush LeBlond was a Maine delegate.

"We were all elected," George W. Bush said proudly. Each announced his state's balloting when the roll call was taken for the presidential nomination.

Two of Bush's three brothers and his sister were also delegates. Brother Jonathan was a New York delegate; brother William "Bucky" Bush was a Missouri delegate; sister Nancy Ellis was a delegate from Massachusetts.

Even George P. Bush, the Vice President's twelve-year-old grandson, the son of Jeb Bush and his wife, Columba, got into the act. As part of the opening ceremonies on the convention's second night, George P. recited the Pledge of Allegiance.

What's the most important gift parents can give to their children? Bush was once asked.

His answer: "Love—that's the most important.

"And then back them up," he said. "When they get hurt, pick them up and dust them off and put them back in the game. You don't leave them when the going is tough.

"Give them a lot of love. They'll come home. Ours have."

CHAPTER THREE

POPPY

His parents, Phillips Academy, and his experience as a navy pilot during World War II made George Bush what he is.

George Bush's parents were Midwesterners who journeyed to New England to make a life for themselves. His father, Prescott, was from Columbus, Ohio. His mother, born Dorothy Walker, came from St. Louis.

Prescott Bush went to college at Yale and, in 1917, when the United States entered World War I, he went into the army. Sent to Europe, he advanced to the rank of captain in the field artillery.

After the war Bush took up a career in business management. His specialty was taking broken-down companies and turning them around, turning them into successes. The family moved frequently as Bush's jobs changed. In 1922, when he was working for the Simmons Hardware Company in Kingsport, Tennessee, his first son, Prescott, Jr., was born.

Two years later Bush was working for the U.S. Rubber Company, and the family lived in Milton, Massachusetts, not far from Boston. That's where George was born. The date: June 12, 1924.

America was a contented nation in those days. Calvin Coolidge, the thirtieth President, was in the White House. Home-run hero Babe Ruth was making headlines for the New York Yankees. Long distance travel was by railroad. The movies were beginning to talk and home television was twenty years away.

The Bush family lived in this house on Adams Street in Milton, Massachusetts, where George was born.
(Wide World)

George was named after his grandfather, George Herbert Walker. (All of the Bush children seemed to have been named after someone.) George once said that his mother couldn't make up her mind which one of her father's names she wanted her second son to have—George Walker or Herbert Walker. She never made a choice. When George was christened, she used them both, naming him George Herbert Walker Bush.

George's mother, Dorothy, called her father Pop. Since George had the same name as grandfather Walker, he came to be called "Little Pop" and "Poppy." That nickname followed him for years. He was Poppy Bush, in fact, when he graduated from Phillips Academy, and the name was used at Yale too. But then it faded away.

The house on Adams Street in Milton where the Bushes lived when George was born is famous now. Reporters and photographers became interested in it after Bush won the presidential election in 1988.

But for years, according to Nina Graves, whose family has lived in the house for about twenty-five years, nobody stopped by—except for an occasion some fifteen years ago when she did get a visitor. It was Bush himself.

Graves once recalled the visit for the Boston *Herald*. "This handsome man said, 'I'm so-and-so and I just wanted to show my son the house I was born in.' I didn't even know who he was."

Graves did not make the connection to the then Vice President until she spoke to a newspaper reporter several years later.

When the U.S. Rubber Company shifted its headquar-

ters from Massachusetts to New York City, the Bushes
moved, too, settling in Greenwich, Connecticut. There the
family lived in a five-bedroom house at 11 Stanwich Road.

George shared a bedroom with his brother Prescott, Jr.,
whom everyone call Pres. Pres was two years older than
George. Despite the difference in their ages, the two
brothers were the best of friends. George was not the kind
of kid who was considered a pest by his older brother.

*George with his sister Dorothy when he was five years old
in 1929.*
(Wide World)

It was pleasant growing up in Greenwich, one of the wealthiest cities in the country. Greenwich boasts mile after mile of huge estates surrounded by stone walls. The homes are visible from the road only during the winter months, when the leaves have fallen from the trees.

In 1931 the Bush family sold the house on Stanwich Road and moved to a bigger house on Grove Lane in Greenwich. A larger house was needed, for the family was growing. Besides George and Pres, it would come to include George's younger brothers Jonathan and Bucky and his sister, Nancy.

A Victorian structure with a huge kitchen, a large dining room, nine bedrooms, and a playroom in the basement, the house had no number when George was growing up. It was simply known as "the Bush house."

In the Bush family, religious training was important. Over breakfast each morning Mr. or Mrs. Bush, solid Episcopalians, read a Bible lesson before the children left for school.

For elementary school, the children attended the Greenwich Country Day School. No school buses took students to the Greenwich Country Day School. It was the kind of place where girls and boys arrived by chauffeured limousine.

The Bush chauffeur was name Alec. At home there were maids and a cook.

The Bushes were a very competitive family. Grandfather Walker was a champion polo player and also excelled at golf. He helped to organize and served as president of the U.S. Golf Association. The Walker Cup is named in his honor. A well-known trophy, the Cup is presented to the winner of a golf competition between amateur men's teams from the United States and Great Britain.

George's father was the amateur golf champion of Ohio and captain of the Yale baseball team. George's mother participated in sports, too. A fine golfer and tennis player, she was known for her even temper, never complaining over a missed putt or poor shot.

It's no wonder the Bush children competed, competed at everything—golf, tennis, table tennis, soccer, backgammon, horseshoes, and even tiddlywinks. And the competition was always very serious.

George's father was an imposing figure. He stood six-foot-four. He had deep-set blue-gray eyes and a deep voice.

Often stiff and stern, Mr. Bush was not the type of father who would give a child a piggyback ride or get down on his hands and knees to put together Lego pieces. He seldom joined in any of the children's sports or games.

It was rare for Mr. Bush to praise one of his children. "You might get a note from him at school," George once stated, "saying something like, 'I was very proud to see that you were elected captain of the team.'"

The note would be signed, "Devotedly, Dad."

Mr. Bush taught his children the importance of public service. "His philosophy about the need to contribute came through quite clearly," Prescott Bush once recalled. "When George talks about that in his speeches, he means it. That's the way we were brought up."

His father's message of sharing and helping others made an impression upon George at an early age. George's

THE BUSH FAMILY TREE

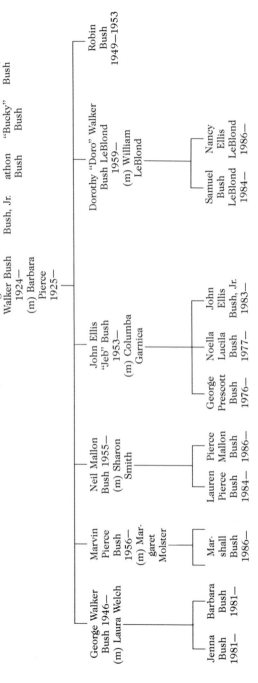

The Bush Family Tree.
(Office of the Vice President)

mother once recalled an obstacle race that took place when he was attending Greenwich Country Day School. One of the obstacles was a barrel that the children had to crawl through. One boy was so fat he got stuck in the barrel. "Everybody broke out laughing," Mrs. Bush recalled. "But George didn't think it was that funny. With tears in his eyes, he went out onto the field and pushed the boy through the barrel."

Although their parents were very well to do, the Bush family members seldom acted as if they were. In fact, growing up was sometimes a penny-pinching experience. Mrs. Bush was very thrifty. "She saved pennies," Jonathan Bush once said, "literally, pennies!"

If one of the children came home late at night and happened to leave a light on, Mrs. Bush would get very upset. And later, when the children were grown and married, and made long-distance telephone calls when visiting, Mrs. Bush would bill each child for his or her calls.

The family belonged to a country club where the children played tennis. But if George or any of the other children wanted a soft drink, they were forbidden to order it at the club. They had to go home and get one out of the refrigerator because it was cheaper.

Humility was another quality that Bush's folks stressed. Bragging was banned. "You could never say how well you played in a game," Jonathan once said.

One day, when George was eight years old, he came home after a tennis match and told his mother he'd been "off his game."

"Off your game?" she said, her brow wrinkling. "You

don't have a game! Get out and work harder and maybe
some day you will."

A writer once described George's father as "the greatest
single influence " on his life. George, in his autobiography, says that this judgment is "only partly right." He says
his mother's influence was just as important as his
father's.

His father, says George, taught him about duty and
responsibility. From his mother he learned the importance of relating to other people, of kindness and
tenderness.

During George's boyhood, the family traveled to South
Carolina for Christmas, where Grandfather Walker owned
a plantation. Often the children would awaken on a freez-
ing morning to the sounds of black servants building pine-
wood fires in bedroom fireplaces.

Each summer the Bush family left Greenwich for Kennebunkport, Maine, specifically for Walker's Point, named
for Grandfather Walker, a piece of rocky land that juts
out into the Atlantic Ocean. The Walker family bought
a rambling twenty-six room home there in 1899, using
it to escape the summer heat.

George has called his summers in Maine "the best of
all possible adventures." The children fished and swam,
and at night George and Pres climbed into a bunk bed
on the screened-in porch, falling asleep to the sound of
the pounding surf.

The most exciting adventures were provided by the
small motorboat, *Tomboy*, which was owned by Grand-

father Walker. He taught George and Pres how to dock
the boat and handle it in the open ocean; he taught them
how to cope with currents, tides, and waves. When Pres
was eleven and George nine, they were given permission
to take the boat out alone, a privilege that made them
the envy of all their friends.

*Today Bush often finds relaxation at the wheel of his power-
boat in the waters of coastal Maine.
(Wide World)*

They fished from the boat for mackerel and pollack using the simplest of equipment—green line wound around a wood rack. Cloth from an old shirt or handkerchief was used as a lure.

When George was older, he advanced from outboard motors to powerboats. In recent years he has enjoyed the pleasures of a twenty-eight-foot Cigaret racing team boat named *Fidelity.* Handling boats is second nature to him now. He has said how much he loves maneuvering through rocky inlets and hidden coves, and traveling across stretches of open ocean with the throttle wide open.

When it came time for George to attend high school, his father picked out Phillips Academy, better known as Andover, after the Massachusetts town in which it is located. Andover is very old, having opened its doors in 1778. Its reputation and its campus are heavy with prestige.

While Andover has always sought to promote a "rigorous academic education," sports are very important. The campus of over five hundred acres offers twenty-five tennis courts, twelve playing fields, and its own ski jump on Holt Hill. The school began admitting girls in 1973. In George's day, it was all male.

While George's grades at Andover were no better than average, in every other aspect of school life he excelled. He was a smooth-fielding first baseman on the baseball team and a star of the soccer team. Indeed, one account of his soccer playing during his senior year at Andover declared: "Poppy Bush's play throughout the season ranked him as one of Andover's all-time greats."

In his senior class yearbook George was ranked among the top four students in five different categories: Best All-Round Fellow, Best Athlete, Most Respected, Most Popular, and Handsomest.

He was also one of the student deacons for Sunday chapel services, and was president of the "S. of I.," the Society of Inquiry, a campus religious group. During the time he was a member of the group, the S. of I. raised

Phillips Academy in Andover, Massachusetts, is one of the oldest and most respected of the eastern prep schools. (Phillips Academy)

GEORGE WALKER BUSH
"POP" "POPPY"
Grove Lane, Greenwich, Conn.

June 12, 1924   Yale

AUV

President of Senior Class (1 term)

Secretary of Student Council (1 term)

Student Council (1941-42)

President of Society of Inquiry (1941-42)

Senior Prom Committee

Chairman of Student Deacons (1941-42)

Advisory Board

President of Greeks (1940-42)

Captain of Baseball (1942)

Captain of Soccer (1941)

Manager of Basketball (1941)

Society of Inquiry (1940-42)

Student Deacon (1940-42)

Editorial Board of the *Phillipian* (1938-39)

All-Club Soccer (1938)

Business Board of the POT POURRI (1940-42)

Deputy Housemaster

Varsity Soccer Squad (1939-41)

Varsity Basketball Team (1941-42)

J.V. Baseball Team (1939)

Varsity Baseball Squad (1940)

Varsity Baseball Team (1941-42)

John Hopkins Prize (1938)

Treasurer of Student Council (1 term)

Bush's yearbook at Andover gives evidence of his many and varied interests.
(Phillips Academy)

money for a Christian medical mission in remote Labrador, a region of northeast Canada.

As a senior, George was involved in some twenty different activities, more than any other student. If he was not *the* most popular boy at Andover, he was surely one of them.

At Andover his classmates began saying something unusual about George Bush. They said he would become President of the United States some day.

CHAPTER FOUR

TROUBLED TIMES

L ate in the summer of 1941 seventeen-year-old George Bush returned to Andover for his senior year. His carefree school days were soon to end.

World War II was raging in Europe. The nations of the world had watched helplessly as the armies of Adolf Hitler had overrun Poland in 1939. Six months later they had struck again, invading and swiftly conquering Denmark and Norway.

In May 1940 German forces launched an assault on Belgium, Luxembourg, and the Netherlands. Within three weeks all three nations were in German hands.

The Germans then knifed into France. In four days the French were in hopeless retreat.

With the fall of France, Great Britain stood alone as the only nation in western Europe not under German control. Hitler boasted that his armies would soon cross the English Channel into Britain.

Hitler, however, decided he would tackle the Soviet Union first. But when German troops invaded Russia, the United States and Britain came to look upon the Soviet Union as an ally and began shipping great quantities of equipment and supplies to the Soviets.

Then, on December 7, 1941, without any declaration of war, Hitler's ally Japan attacked the U.S. naval base at Pearl Harbor, Hawaii. Japanese bombers killed and wounded thousands of Americans that day.

With the United States suddenly thrust into the war, young men and women by the millions volunteered to serve in the army, navy, Marine Corps, and Coast Guard. George Bush was one of them. "The whole country was so together, so unified, that I was swept into it," Bush has said.

George not only wanted to enlist, he had even made up his mind which branch of the service he would enter. He wanted to become a naval aviator.

But George's parents didn't think enlisting was a very good idea. His mother tried to talk him out of it but without any success. George did agree, however, to postpone the move until he had graduated from Andover.

George's reasons for going into the service went beyond simple patriotism. "I had a very powerful father," Bush once said, "very much of a leader, admired by everybody. I had a kind of—not really a competitive thing with him—but I wanted to get out on my own."

Certainly, enlisting in the navy was a chance for

George to do something on his own. It was an opportunity to "get out from under," to seek his own identity.

Early in June 1942 Secretary of War Henry Stimson journeyed from Washington to Andover to deliver the commencement address. He told George and the other members of the graduating class that he believed the war was going to be a long one. And he said that even though the United States needed fighting men, they could serve

The Japanese attack on the U.S. naval base at Pearl Harbor, Hawaii, on December 7, 1941, plunged the United States into World War II.
(U.S. Navy)

their country better by getting more education before signing up with the military.

After the address George, who was set to attend Yale in the fall, spoke with his father outside of Cochran Chapel.

"George," his father asked, "did the Secretary say anything to change your mind?"

"No sir," said George, "I'm going in."

His father noddded, then shook George's hand.

On June 12, 1942, his eighteenth birthday, George went to Boston to be sworn into the navy as a seaman second class, the first step toward becoming a naval aviation cadet in those days. Not long after, his dad put him on a crowded train at Penn Station in New York. The train headed south to Chapel Hill, North Carolina, for preflight training.

George was younger than the other trainees. In fact, when he got his wings, he would be described as the youngest aviator in the navy.

George had enlisted in the navy a week before the Battle of Midway in the northern Pacific Ocean, the first important naval battle in history in which surface ships —battleships, cruisers, and destroyers—had no combat role. The Battle of Midway was a battle of aircraft carriers. A new era was dawning. The navy wanted more planes and the pilots to fly them, and it wanted them fast.

George's class was rushed through preflight training at Chapel Hill, and then sent to Wold Chamberlain Naval Air Station at Minneapolis for primary flight training. The student pilots learned to fly in an open-cockpit trainer. Their equipment included face masks to protect them against the bitter Minnesota cold. Even so, some of the

At the time George won his commission as an ensign, he was the navy's youngest pilot.
(U.S. Navy)

students ended up with frostbitten faces. George and the other cadets who passed the course were happy to be sent to the warm sunshine of Corpus Christi, Texas, for the next phase of training.

In June of 1943 George earned his wings and soon after became a navy ensign. He was still eighteen.

A few months later, in August, George took another important step—he got engaged. Her name was Barbara Pierce. She had grown up in Rye, New York, just north of New York City, the daughter of a magazine publisher. "She had the benefit of a good family, good education, and good breeding," *Ladies Home Journal* once noted.

The two had met at a Christmas dance the year before. The band was playing Glenn Miller-type music. Since George didn't dance, they had to sit and talk, and thus it didn't take very long for them to get to know each other.

Of that first meeting Barbara has said, "I thought he was the most beautiful creature I had ever laid eyes on. I couldn't even breathe when he was in the room."

Their relationship advanced quickly from simply being "serious" to the point where they were meeting and spending time with one another's families, a practice that George has described as being "a fairly important step for teenagers in those days."

In the summer of 1943 Barbara joined the Bush family in Maine, and that's when the couple became engaged. The engagement was formally announced that December.

The early 1940s were times of great uncertainty for young people. One half of the world seemed to be fighting the other half. Barbara and George realized that marriage was years away.

CHAPTER FIVE

BAILOUT

In the fall of 1943 Ensign George Bush resumed flight training at Fort Lauderdale, Florida, and Chincoteague, Virginia. He had been assigned to torpedo bombers.

Torpedo bombing is glide bombing, diving down and then cruising in at low altitude to launch one's torpedo toward an enemy ship. Torpedo bombers also carried and dropped conventional bombs. And sometimes they were used to provide air support for troops engaged in amphibious landings by spraying enemy positions with machine-gun fire.

Once he had completed flight training, Bush was assigned to the U.S.S. *San Jacinto*, an aircraft carrier. From the carrier's deck George made practice bombing runs on targets up and down the east coast of the United States.

The *San Jacinto* had originally been planned as a cruiser. But heavily gunned warships such as cruisers and battleships weren't needed in the vast stretches of the Pacific. Aircraft carriers were. So the navy ordered a flight deck built atop the cruiser's keel.

As a navy pilot, Bush served aboard the U.S.S. San Jacinto, a light aircraft carrier.
(U.S. Navy)

After the sinking of the U.S.S. *Houston* in the Dutch East Indies early in 1943, the citizens of Houston bought enough war bonds to provide funds to build a replacement ship—the *San Jacinto*. (It was at the Battle of San Jacinto that Texas, under the leadership of Sam Houston, defeated the Mexicans, thereby achieving independence from Mexico.)

Although top-heavy and lightly armed, the *San Jacinto* was fast, capable of carrying its thirty-five planes at a top speed of thirty-five knots (or about thirty-nine miles per hour).

In the spring of 1944 the *San Jacinto* eased its way through the Panama Canal, then headed west across the Pacific to operate as one of the eight fast carriers in Task Force 58. Aboard the *San Jacinto* Bush piloted a TBM Avenger, a chunky, single-engine midwing plane with a powerful engine. Bush had Barbara's name painted on his plane's nose.

The Avenger was the first aircraft of its type capable of carrying a 2,000-pound torpedo or bombs of equivalent weight. It was not, however, a fast plane; in fact, pilots of the day described it as "low and slow." And one crew member said the Avenger "could fall faster than it could fly." Cruising speed was around 140 knots. It landed at about 95 knots.

Bush liked flying the Avenger, liked the challenge it offered, the thrill of diving down at full speed, pulling out, and gliding close to the water.

At first he shuddered at the idea of landing on the carrier's deck. From the air the narrow deck looked no big-

ger than a throw rug. It took total concentration—gliding
in, watching the landing-signal officer who waved bright-
ly colored paddles to let the pilot know whether he was
too high, too low, or right on target. Then the idea was
to ease the plane down until he felt the wheels touch and
the tailhook catch the arresting cable stretched across

San Jacinto's *flight deck was built atop a cruiser's keel.*
(U.S. Navy)

the deck, which brought the plane to a jolting stop.

The slightest mistake could be disastrous. Bush knew that.

One day, after bringing his plane back to the ship following a bombing run, Bush was standing on the *San Jacinto's* flight deck watching other planes land. A fight-

er plane came roaring in, and its tailhook missed the cable. The pilot gunned the engine, trying to get airborne again. But the plane spun out of control and slammed into a gun position on the deck that was manned by four sailors. All four were wiped out.

It all happened in the blink of an eye. Never before had George seen death strike so suddenly. Never before had it come so close.

As American forces island-hopped their way across the Pacific toward Japan, the aircraft from the *San Jacinto*

A Grumman Avenger, the torpedo bomber Bush flew during World War II.
(U.S. Navy)

were often assigned to provide low-level protection for land forces. Other times the Avengers would fly glide-bombing raids on land targets. Still other times the planes would be armed with depth charges and be sent out on antisubmarine patrol.

George flew low-level air cover through heavy antiaircraft fire when American forces landed on the central Pacific islands of Guam and Saipan. "We could see the troops going ashore and the big guns from the battleships firing over them," Bush recalls, "and all I could do was count my blessings that I was up there instead of down below."

In the middle of June 1944, the Japanese launched a massive air strike against American ships clustered in the northern Pacific east of the Philippines near Guam, Saipan, and other of the Mariana Islands. More than three hundred enemy aircraft were involved in the attack.

The *San Jacinto* was one of the targets. When the *San Jacinto*'s fighter planes rose up to engage the Japanese aircraft, Bush and the other Avenger pilots were also sent into the air so their planes would not be lined up like sitting ducks on the carrier's flight deck.

As George's plane was about to be launched, he realized he had engine trouble. A gauge on the instrument panel indicated there was no oil pressure. But it was too late to halt the launch. George's Avenger was hurtled into the air from the ship's catapult.

George was airborne only a few minutes when the engine began to sputter. George was cool. He took the plane up ahead of the fleet and circled low over the water, preparing to ditch. What worried him and his two crew members was the fact that the plane was carrying four 500-pound depth charges. How does one plop a lumbering bomber into the water with 500-pound bombs in its belly? George has been asked this question many times.

His answer: "Very carefully."

George brought the plane down low, almost skimming the waves. Before he set it down, he pulled the nose up, just as he had been trained to do in flight school. The tail touched the water first and skidded over the surface. Then George dropped the nose—a beautiful landing.

The three men scrambled out onto the wing, got their raft inflated, climbed into it, and started paddling. As the plane sank out of sight, the depth charges exploded.

Soon after, the three men were picked up by a destroyer. They were back aboard the *San Jacinto* a few days later.

In the weeks that followed, George and the other Avenger pilots continued to fly antisubmarine patrols and attack enemy-held island strongholds. On September 1, 1944, Bush's squadron of Avengers struck at radio communication centers on Chichi Jima, one of the Bonin Islands, about six hundred miles south of the Japanese mainland. They were met with fierce antiaircraft fire.

When the planes got back to their ship, the radio stations were still operating. The pilots knew they would have to return the next day and finish the job.

Early the next morning, as George prepared for the mission, Ted White, the gunnery officer aboard the *San Jacinto* and a friend of George's, asked him whether he could go along on the raid as the turret gunner. White said he wanted to check out the Avenger's equipment under combat conditions.

George said it was all right with him if the commanding officer approved. Once approval was granted, White joined Bush and Jack Delaney, the young radioman/gunner, in Bush's Avenger.

The plane took off on schedule. Once airborne, they were joined by three other Avengers from the *San Jacinto*, plus more than a dozen fighters. Each of the Avengers carried four 500-pound bombs.

Over Chichi Jima, the sky was filled with black clumps of exploding antiaircraft fire. Bush could not recall having ever flown in such intense flak.

The squadron commander led the first pair of attacking bombers, scoring direct hits on a radio tower and damaging other buildings. George and another Avenger were to go next. As he put his plane into a dive, George felt a sudden jolt. Antiaircraft fire had hit his engine. Thick black smoke poured toward the cockpit. Flames licked the wings. But Bush did not panic. He kept the plane in its dive, unloaded the bombs, and then pulled away.

For his bravery, George would later receive the Distinguished Flying Cross. The citation reads:

> Opposed by intense antiaircraft fire, his plane was hit and set afire as he commenced his dive. In spite of smoke and flames from the fire in his plane, he continued his dive and scored damaging bomb hits on the radio station before bailing out of his plane. His courage and com-

plete disregard for his own safety, both in press-
ing home his attack in the face of intense and
accurate anti-aircraft fire and in continuing his
dive on the target after being hit and his plane
on fire, were at all times in keeping with the
highest traditions of the United States Naval
Service.

There is more to the story, much more. Realizing that
his plane was crippled, Bush headed toward open ocean.
Using the intercom, he told White and Delaney to bail
out. Neither man responded; George leveled the plane
to make it easier for them to jump. Then he checked his
parachute and plunged over the side.

A couple of things went wrong. He banged his head on
the tail and he pulled the parachute ripcord before he
should have. As a result, his chute caught on the tail. Luck-
ily, it tore free. Although he went down fast, he still
managed to get out of his parachute harness after landing and swim to his seat-pack life raft.

As he sat in the raft, he scanned the gray-green water
for some sign of his two crew members, White and
Delaney. He saw nothing. Even the sky was empty. The
other planes were already on their way back to the *San
Jacinto*. Bush was alone.

The raft began to drift toward Chichi Jima. George pad-
dled with both hands to keep it away from the enemy-
held island.

His head was bleeding from the blow he suffered when
he collided with the plane's tail. He kept paddling. An hour
passed, two hours. His head ached. His arms ached. He

got sick from salt water he had swallowed and started throwing up.

"It seemed," he has said, "just the end of the world."

Suddenly, just a few hundred feet away, a small black dot appeared. The dot got bigger. Then George recognized the dot as a submarine periscope. The submarine's conning tower broke the water's surface, and then moments later the entire hull was before him. It was the submarine U.S.S. *Finback,* George's rescue ship. He later learned that the planes in his squadron had radioed the position of his raft to the *Finback.*

Within minutes, George was aboard the sub. Then the hatches slammed shut, a loud horn blared, and the skipper gave the order to "Take her down!" George silently thanked God for having saved his life.

He also prayed for the safety of his crewmates. Later he learned that only one crewman was seen jumping from the plane but his parachute never fully opened. The other crewman plunged into the sea with the plane. Whether this crewman was hit by gunfire and unable to get out, Bush still does not know. Nor does he know which crew member it was, Ted White or radioman John Delaney.

Aboard the *Finback* were three other navy fliers who had been rescued just as George had. Like George, they were eager to be reunited with their squadrons. But the reunions were going to have to wait. The *Finback* was a combat ship on patrol. It had to complete its tour of duty before dropping off the rescued pilots.

George lived aboard the *Finback* for a month. He will never forget the day the sub was attacked by a Japanese bomber and he learned what it is like to be depth-charged. It wasn't a pleasant experience. "That depth-charging got to me," he says. "It just shook the boat, and those guys would say, 'Oh, that wasn't close.'" It was close enough for George. It shook him up.

There is a footnote to George Bush's ordeal under fire. In the summer of 1988, as Bush campaigned for the presidency, his account of the events of September 2,

Submarine Finback *came to Bush's rescue when his plane was downed at sea.*
(U.S. Navy)

1944, was questioned. The questioner was 68-year-old Chester Mierzejewski, a retired aircraft factory worker foreman who lived in Cheshire, Connecticut. Mierzejewski had been the turret gunner in the Avenger piloted by Bush's squadron commander. At the time Bush's plane was struck by antiaircraft fire, Mierzejewski's plane was about 100 feet ahead of Bush's plane.

After Bush's plane was hit, Mierzejewski saw a "puff of smoke," according to an article that appeared in the New

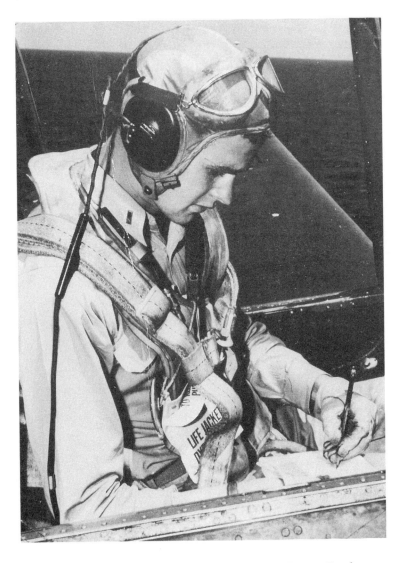

*For his bravery during a bombing mission, Lieut. Bush was
awarded the Distinguished Flying Cross.
(The White House)*

York *Post* in August 1988. But the smoke quickly cleared away, and then no more smoke appeared. Bush's "plane was never on fire," Mierzejewski declared.

If Mierzejewski's account of the tragedy was true, why did Bush bail out? If there was no fire, why didn't he land the plane on the water? With a water landing, he would have increased the chances of survival for the entire three-man crew.

Mierzejewski also stated that only one man parachuted from the plane—and that was Bush.

"I saw the plane go down" said Mierzejewski. "I knew the guys were still in it."

Mierzejewski wrote Bush a letter telling him that his recollections of the incident were "entirely different" from Bush's. There was no reply to the letter.

But Steve Hart, the Vice President's press secretary at the time, had this to say: "The Vice President has told us time and time again what happened that day. To suggest that his account is inaccurate is absurd."

Eight weeks after being shot down, George was back aboard the *San Jacinto*. American and Australian forces were edging closer and closer to the Japanese mainland. Late in October 1944, more than 100,000 American troops, supported by invasion armada, landed on Leyte, one of the Japanese-held Philippine Islands. American B-29 bombers by the hundreds, taking off from bases in Saipan and Guam, kept Tokyo and other cities of the Japanese home islands under constant attack.

George, at the controls of a new Avenger, took part in

the air strikes against enemy ground installations and shipping in the Philippines. In December that year he was
ordered home. By then he had racked up 1,228 hours in
the air, 126 carrier landings, and 58 combat missions.

George got home in time for Christmas. It was a time
of mixed feelings for Americans. The happiness of the
holiday season was tainted by the lengthening lists of
names of those killed, wounded, and missing in the battle zones of the Pacific and Europe. "There were a lot of
tears, and a lot of hugging," George recalls. "The war had
been dragging on for more than three years. The end still
seemed far away."

Not long after Christmas, on January 6, 1945, George
and Barbara Pierce were married at the First Presbyterian Church in her hometown of Rye, New York. George
wore his blue uniform; she, an elegant white gown.

Now they were like millions of other young couples,
shuffling by bus or train from one military post to another.
George was sent to Florida and then Michigan for retrain-
ing. The navy planned to assign him to another aircraft
carrier for the final assault on the Japanese mainland.
Like many Americans, George felt it was going to be the
bloodiest battle of the war.

By the summer of 1945 Germany had surrendered to
the Western Allies and the Soviet Union. George was sta-
tioned at Virginia Beach, Virginia, flying out of the Oceana
Naval Air Station. Barbara was with him. They were there
when they heard the news that President Harry Truman
had ordered atomic bombs to be dropped on the Japanese
cities of Hiroshima and Nagasaki. About a week later the
war was over.

Today Bush has no patience with critics who question President Truman's decision to use nuclear weapons against the Japanese. "It wasn't just courageous," Bush has said, "it was farsighted." Bush says that millions of fighting men on both sides would have been killed. "He spared the world and the Japanese people an unimaginable holocaust," Bush states in his autobiography.

When the announcement of the war's end came, George, Barbara, and other pilots and their wives started to celebrate. But George and Barbara first went to church to give thanks. Then they joined the thousands who poured into the streets of Virginia Beach. They jumped and yelled like kids.

The war was over. The killing had stopped. They were free to lead normal lives again.

CHAPTER SIX

THE
TEXAS YEARS

After George Bush was released from active duty in the navy in September 1945, there was no doubt what he would do. He would go to Yale. His father had gone there. His older brother and several nephews had gone there. Going to Yale was a family tradition.

George and Barbara moved into a basement apartment in New Haven, Connecticut, where Yale is located. Bush majored in economics, as he had at Andover, and again was very active in sports. He played one season of soccer, a year in which the team won the New England collegiate championship.

George was a smooth-fielding first baseman on the Yale baseball team.
(Yale University)

Baseball, however, was Bush's favorite sport. He was a first baseman who quickly won a reputation as a slick fielder. Junie O'Brien, a teammate of Bush's, once said: "The thing about Poppy—as everyone called him—was that he was so sure-gloved. All the infielders knew that if they threw the ball anywhere near him, he was going to pull it in."

As a hitter, however, Bush won little acclaim. In 1947 his average was .239. The next season he was better, batting .264.

Yale had an outstanding baseball team in the years Bush played. In both 1947 and 1948 Yale was runner-up in the National Collegiate Athletic Association championships. Three of Bush's teammates were signed by major league teams. It was Bush, however, who was elected team captain.

Because he wanted to graduate as quickly as possible, Bush took courses during vacation periods. This enabled him to graduate in two and a half years. He was awarded Phi Beta Kappa honors, evidence that he was a top student.

Another hint of Bush's future success came on "tap night," when the standout members of the incoming class are inducted into Yale's secret societies. According to the ritual, the best candidates are the last to be chosen, and Bush was the very last to be tapped, an indication he was considered the most desirable man in his class.

Bush became a father while at Yale. In July 1946 the Bushes' first child, a boy, was born. They named him George, Jr.

At the time Bush graduated from Yale in 1948, his father was a partner in Brown Brothers, Harriman and Company, one of the most successful investment banking firms of the day. Although a policy was in force that prohibited the hiring of relatives, the company was willing to make an exception in George's case, and he was offered a job. But he said no.

George had other plans. He had saved three thousand dollars in the navy, enough, he felt, to get him and Barbara and George, Jr., started on their own. And getting started on his own was what he wanted to do. He wanted to break away, to begin shaping his own future.

He did, however, turn to a close family friend, Neil Henry Mallon, who lent a helping hand. Mallon was president of Dresser Industries, a huge oil company. He had no children and George was almost like a son to him.

GEORGE HERBERT WALKER BUSH (Poppy) was born in Milton, Mass., June 12, 1924. He is the son of Prescott Sheldon Bush, '17, and Dorothy Walker Bush, a brother of Prescott S. Bush, Jr., *ex*-'44, and a nephew of James S. Bush, '22, George H. Walker, Jr., '27, John M. Walker, '31, and Louis Walker, '36.

In 1942, after graduating from Andover, Bush entered Naval Aviation. He later served as pilot in the Pacific and was awarded the D.F.C. He was discharged as a lieutenant (j.g.) in September, 1945, and entered Yale in November. Bush, who has majored in economics, was awarded the Francis Gordon Brown Prize in 1947. He was on the University baseball team for three years, being captain in Senior year, and on the University soccer team in 1945; he has both a minor and major "Y." He was secretary of the 1946 Budget drive and in 1947 served on the Undergraduate Athletic Association, the Undergraduate Board of Deacons, and the Interfraternity Council and was elected to the Triennial Committee. He belongs to Delta Kappa Epsilon, the Torch Honor Society, and Skull and Bones.

He was married in Rye, N. Y., January 6, 1945, to Barbara Pierce, Smith *ex*-'47, daughter of Marvin and Pauline Robinson Pierce. Their son, George Walker, was born in New Haven, July 6, 1946. Bush may be addressed at Grove Lane, Greenwich, Conn.

At Yale George was an honor student, active in sports and many other activities.
(Yale University)

(Bush would later name one of his sons after Mallon.) Remembering that George had lived in Texas, in Corpus Christi, during his navy career, Mallon made a suggestion. "What you need to do is head out to Texas and those oil fields," he said. "That's the place for ambitious young people these days."

Mallon backed up his suggestion with a job offer. Ideco (short for the International Derrick and Equipment Company), a subsidiary of Dresser Industries, had an opening for a trainee in West Texas. It didn't pay much, Mallon explained, but it was a chance to learn the oil business.

Did George want the job? Indeed he did.

He packed up his red Studebaker and headed for Texas. Barbara and their young son would join him after he found a place to live.

In 1948 west Texas was in the midst of the great Scurry County oil boom. Thousands of workers flocked to the area. Housing was so scarce in Midland and Odessa that tent cities had sprung up.

George found a place for the family to live in Odessa, a small, shabby house on East Seventh Street with a flimsy partition down the middle that divided it into two apartments. They had a bedroom, a small kitchen, a shared bathroom with the woman tenant on the other side of the partition.

An Ideco supervisor named Bill Nelson, warm and friendly but with a gruff exterior, was George's boss. He taught George the language of the oil fields, explaining that the products Ideco sold could be summed up as "soap, rope, and dope." Soap was what Ideco's customers used to clean the drilling rigs. Rope was the wire line used for hoisting. And dope was the stuff the drillers put on the threads of drill pipe, tubing, and casing.

Learning to talk like an oil-field worker was only the beginning of George's education. More important, he learned about oil royalties, about property laws and land leases. It was knowledge he knew he would put to work in the future.

Nelson put George to work sweeping warehouses and painting machinery. Bush asked questions until Nelson got tired of answering them, and he never stopped working. Before Nelson went home at night, he would put a list of things to do on George's desk. By the time Nelson arrived the next day, George would have already done them.

Over the years Nelson trained hundreds of young men for Ideco. "George was better than any of 'em," he says.

In less than a year George was made an Ideco salesman and transferred to California. He was on the road from one end of the week to the other selling drilling bits, the boring heads used for drilling wells. The family lived in Whittier, then Ventura, the Compton. In Compton in 1949, the Bushes' second child and first daughter was born, named Robin.

The Bushes returned to Texas in 1950, settling in Midland. By now Bush was caught up in the excitement of the booming oil business. But he wanted to be more involved than he was permitted to be by his job at Ideco.

With a Midland neighbor, John Overby, Bush set up the Bush-Overby Oil Development Company. But he first spoke to Neil Mallon, who had hired him as an Ideco trainee some two and a half years before. He explained

During his Texas years Bush developed a great fondness for Mexican food. Here, as Vice President, he eats a tamale the proper way—with his fingers.
(Wide World)

to Mallon that he had "caught the fever," that he wanted to become an independent oilman.

Mallon understood how George felt. "I really hate to see you go, George," he said. "But if I were your age, I'd be doing the same thing."

Independent oilmen are oil deal promoters. They try to convince landowners to sell them what's beneath the surface of their land, the mineral rights, the oil and gas. As payment, the promoter gets a free share of the deal.

The next step is to find investors to finance the drilling. If oil or gas is found on the leased property, the investors get a percentage of the income. So does the landowner. If nothing is found, the investors lose their money.

Bush crisscrossed the state of Texas in search of farmers and ranchers willing to sell him their mineral rights. Sometimes his quest took him beyond the borders of Texas, and once he trekked as far north as North Dakota.

He spent an equal amount of time scouring big cities for investors. Bush's uncle, Herbie Walker, helped him with funds at the beginning. But Bush had the knack of being able to attract money from many other investors besides his relatives and friends.

At the same time, Bush, his wife, and their friends sought "to give something back" to their fast-growing community. Bush coached boys' baseball and helped get the YMCA and a community health center started. He taught Sunday school, was an elder of the First Presbyterian Church, and served as a director of the Midland Bank. His wife once recalled that so many people made demands upon George's time that she was sometimes jealous.

By 1953 the Bushes' fortunes had improved sharply. The improvement enabled Bush to join with three other partners in forming the Zapata Petroleum Corporation, which took over Bush-Overby. In 1956 Bush became president of a Zapata subsidiary, the Zapata Offshore Company, which pioneered in the development of offshore drilling equipment. The Bushes moved to Houston, where the company had its headquarters, in 1958. When Bush sold out his interest in Zapata in 1966, the sale made him a millionaire.

But just as the Bushes seemed to have their lives on a successful track, tragedy struck. One morning their daughter Robin woke listless and weak. A doctor did some tests. They showed that Robin was a very sick child. She had leukemia, a cancerous disease of the blood. Robin had only six months to live, doctors said.

The Bushes took Robin to a hospital in New York City for treatment. But it was in vain. Robin was three years and ten months old when she died.

"Barbara and I sustained each other, but in the end it was our faith that truly sustained us," Bush wrote in his autobiography. "To this day, like every parent who ever lost a child, we wonder why; yet we know that whatever the reason, she is in God's loving arms."

Three other children were born to the Bushes during their Midland years—John Ellis (Jeb), Neil Mallon, and Marvin Pierce. Dorothy ("Doro") Walker was born in 1959. But by that time the Bushes were living in Houston.

The Bushes with their children in 1964; from left, back row, Neil, George, and John; front row, Dorothy and Marvin. (The White House)

Bush has fond memories of the years the family lived in Midland. In 1988, when campaigning for the presidency, Bush returned to the city and spoke in warm terms about his life there some thirty years before. "We were all chiseling for a buck in those days," he said. "And we had great fun there. I loved my long drives as an oilfield salesman...and I can still remember the chili from that pool hall downtown....The great barbecue from Johnny's is still here....This is where our boys were born, Midland hospital...and this is where on Sunday, you know, the cookout bit after church, and this is where Barbara got started on her world record—I think she still holds it—as the mother that watched the most Little League games."

CHAPTER SEVEN
BORN TO RUN

George Bush had gone to Texas as a man of 25 to seek his fortune in the oil business. But by the time he was 35, he felt he had achieved everything that he had hoped to achieve. He had built a company from the ground up. His investments had paid off. The company was thriving.

He was no longer thinking of just business success. More and more he was beginning to be attracted by a career in politics.

In the years that Bush was growing up in Greenwich, Connecticut, the Bushes were not much of a political family. Although his father was a Republican and was sometimes active in helping raise funds for the party, the topic of politics was rarely raised at family gatherings.

Bush's father, Prescott, entered the political arena in 1950 at the age of 55 by running for a seat in the Senate. By this time George Bush had left home for Midland, Texas.

Bush fully understood his father's plans. "It didn't surprise me," Bush said in his autobiography, "because I knew what motivated him. He'd made his mark in the business world. Now he felt he had a debt to pay."

A newspaper reporter covering the 1950 Senate race expressed it in these terms: "Pres has an old-fashioned idea that the more advantages a man has, the greater the obligation to do public service."

Prescott Bush faced Democrat William Benton, who was already serving in the Senate, in the 1950 race. George's father lost by only 1,000 votes out of the 862,000 cast, a very strong showing for a first-time candidate.

Mr. Bush's political philosophy put him in opposition to old-line, conservative Republicans. He represented a more practical approach to domestic and international problems, and he supported Dwight D. Eisenhower in his successful bid to win the Republican presidential nomination against the forces of Senator Robert A. Taft.

When Connecticut's senior senator, Brien McMahon, a Democrat, died in 1952, the Republicans nominated Prescott Bush to run in a special election to fill the vacancy. This time Mr. Bush won, defeating Abraham Ribicoff. Senator Bush was re-elected in 1956.

Altogether, Prescott Bush served ten years in the Senate, retiring in 1962. That was about the same time that George decided to follow in his father's footsteps, and launched his own career.

George's first job in politics was as party chairman for the Republican party in Harris County, Texas, which includes the city of Houston. At the time, Texas was very much a Democratic state. Republicans were a rare breed.

Old-line Democrats still blamed the Republicans for the Great Depression, which began in 1929 and continued deep into the 1930s. Millions of people had been thrown out of work. Farmers and ranchers had lost their homes and land to banks and other mortgage holders. Older Democrats believed the nation had been rescued by Franklin D. Roosevelt and the Democratic party.

But at about the time the Bushes had arrived in Texas, the Democrats were beginning to have difficulties. A split had developed between liberal Democrats and conservative Democrats. The division had weakened the party.

On the other hand, the Republicans were showing signs of life. When Republican Dwight D. Eisenhower won the presidency in 1952 and 1956, he carried the state of Texas by big margins both times.

Bush, as Republican party chairman in Harris County, preached a gospel stressing the value of the two-party system. The Republican party, he declared, offered the Texas voter an alternative to the old-line Democrats. By the end of 1963 the Republicans were showing surprising growth.

In 1964 George ran for a seat in the U.S. Senate. His opponent was Ralph Yarborough, who then held the office. Although Bush lost, he managed to capture 43.5 percent of the vote, a larger share than any other Republican candidate in Texas history.

Most of Bush's business associates were baffled by what he was doing. They couldn't understand how he could give up his privacy and the chance to earn a fortune in the oil business for a career in politics. It didn't make sense to them.

But Bush loved it. When he campaigned, he was a bun-

dle of energy and enthusiasm. If he had ten or fifteen
minutes between speeches, he'd go out and shake people's hands. He'd be up at six A.M., often delivering coffee
to the rooms of his staff members.

"In Midland I was bitten by the bug that led me into
the oil busines," he said. "Now I'd been bitten by another
bug."

George Bush
U.S. Senator
Houston

With a strong conservative political philosophy that meshes closely
with the beliefs of Barry Gold-
water, John Tower, and Bruce
Alger, George Bush will give Texas
another strong, clear voice in support of integrity, states rights, a
foreign policy based on unmatched
military strength, and a private
enterprise economy unhampered
by bureaucratic meddling.

*When Bush run for the Senate in 1964, a campaign brochure
described him as having "a strong conservative political
philosophy."*
(From the collection of David Quintin)

In February 1966, fifteen months after he had been defeated in the race for the U.S. Senate by Ralph Yarborough, Bush resigned as Chairman and Chief Executive Officer of the Zapata Offshore Company to devote full time to his career in politics. He now had his eye on a seat in the House of Representatives for Texas' Seventh Congressional District, which included one of Houston's wealthiest neighborhoods.

Bush was opposed by Frank Briscoe, a conservative Democrat. Briscoe's views and Bush's were not very different. Both men supported President Lyndon Johnson's policies in Vietnam and both promised to work to cut federal spending.

The decision for the voters was based largely on which of the two candidates would be the stronger voice in Washington. Bush's posters and campaign literature pictured him in shirtsleeves, a coat slung over one shoulder. ELECT GEORGE BUSH TO CONGRESS AND WATCH THE ACTION! they declared.

Thanks to that campaign theme—and plenty of hard work—Bush won easily, becoming the first Republican to represent Houston in Congress. Two years later, in 1968, Bush was elected without any Democratic opposition.

When Bush arrived in Washington early in 1967 to begin life as a freshman Congressman, the nation was in turmoil. Vietnam was the reason. Beginning in the late 1940s, the United States had been sending aid to South Vietnam as that nation struggled to fight off a takeover by the Communist North Vietnamese. North Vietnam was supported by the Soviet Union and China.

Joyous Bush hugs his daughter Dorothy after winning race
for a seat in the House of Representatives in 1966.
(Wide World)

In 1964 the United States began air strikes against North Vietnam, and the following year American troops became involved in the fighting there. As President Lyndon B. Johnson stepped up the bombing and ordered more and more American fighting men to Vietnam, he saw his popularity begin to wane. As the war dragged on and the casualties mounted, the nation's resistance stiffened. By the time Johnson left office in 1969, close to half a million U.S. troops were in Vietnam, and angry war protestors were marching on the White House, hurling bitter slogans and insults at L.B.J.

In 1967 Bush supported the Vietnam War (later, he came out in favor of withdrawing American troops). Bush favored fair-housing legislation, although it was unpopular in his district. He had a strong interest in population control and legislation concerning the environment. He was a loyal spokesman for the oil industry.

Through his father's influence, Bush was given a seat on the Ways and Means Committee of the House of Representatives, a rare honor for a first-year Congressman. All tax legislation originates with the House Ways and Means Committee. Bush called it "the most powerful committee in the House."

From the beginning, Bush sought to establish friendly relations with President Johnson, a fellow Texan. Earlier, as a Senator, Johnson had enjoyed a good relationship with Bush's father during the years he represented the state of Connecticut in the Senate. In fact, Prescott Bush and Lyndon Johnson had served together on the Senate Armed Services Committee.

When Bush received a letter from a White House aide welcoming him to the Congress, Bush wrote in response that "coming from Texas, I am determined not to be a personal embarrassment to our President.

"I recognize the tremendous burden he has," Bush's letter continued, "and will try to be respectful in agreement and disagreement."

In the presidential election of 1968, Richard Nixon was

Although a Republican, Bush sought to establish a close relationship with President Lyndon B. Johnson, a Democrat. This photo was taken early in 1969, not long after L.B.J. had left office.
(Lyndon Baines Johnson Library)

the nation's choice. On inauguration day, as Republicans celebrated, Bush headed out to Andrews Air Force Base to bid Johnson farewell. Members of Johnson's family were there along with a handful of friends. The President went down the line shaking hands. Bush was the only Republican present.

After his reelection to Congress in 1968, Bush was looked upon as a bright star in the Republican party. He sought to keep his star on the rise by establishing close ties with President Nixon.

Bush managed to get an invitation to Nixon's home in San Clemente, California, to make a presentation to the President and some of his advisers on the subject of tax relief for independent oil drillers. Since Bush had once been an independent oil driller himself, he was considered something of an expert.

Bush was in good form. John D. Ehrlichman, a Nixon aide, recently praised Bush's performance that day in an article in the Washington *Post*. "Bush really showed up in that meeting; he was articulate and he argued the merits," said Ehrlichman. "When he left, he had won Richard Nixon's heart and soul."

Nixon had plans for George. He wanted him to run for the U.S. Senate seat then held by Bush's old rival Ralph Yarborough.

But George was undecided about whether to do what Nixon wanted. He knew that his seat in the House of Representatives was a "safe" seat, that the voters in the district he represented were certain to return him to Congress in 1970. In 1968 the Democrats had not even bothered to run a candidate against him.

Running for the Senate, however, represented a risk, even though Yarborough seemed much easier to beat now than he had when George faced him in 1964. Still, George knew that if he lost he'd be out of a job.

Bush went to see Lyndon Johnson at his ranch in Stonewall, Texas, to ask his advice. Johnson, who had served in both the Senate and the House, explained that there was no comparison between the two institutions. The Senate, he said, meant power and prestige; the House didn't. Not long after, Bush announced he was running for the Senate.

It was during this period that Bush became close friends with Jim Baker, whom he had met in the late 1950s. It has been said that without Baker, George Bush would never have become President. And that Baker, without Bush, would never have entered politics or government.

Both dedicated tennis players, the two men became doubles partners (and club champions) at the elegant Houston Country Club. They were neighbors in the exclusive River Oaks section of Houston. A corporate lawyer with a firm that represented oil and gas clients, Baker had many of the same values and interests as Bush. Both had graduated from exclusive colleges in the Northeast, Bush from Yale, Baker from Princeton. Both had been in the service, Bush in the navy, Baker in the Marine Corps.

Baker was going through a difficult time. His wife had recently died of cancer, leaving him with four young children. Bush went out of his way to be a friend to Baker and try to comfort him. He urged Baker to give him a hand in his campaign for the Senate, and Baker pitched in. It was the beginning of a friendship that was to stretch more than thirty years and have an important influence on both men's lives.

In the 1970 Senate race Bush's strategy was to pit his conservative views against Yarborough's liberalism. President Nixon promised to give Bush his all-out support, and

You and your family are invited
to see and hear

THE PRESIDENT OF THE UNITED STATES

Richard M. Nixon

speaking in behalf of

CONGRESSMAN GEORGE BUSH, *Candidate for U.S. Senate*

PAUL W. EGGERS, *Candidate for Governor*

Wednesday, October 28, 1970

3:30 p.m.   Gregg County Airport — Longview

President Nixon journeyed to Texas to campaign for Bush in 1970.
(From the collection of Ron Wade)

Bush knew his oil-industry friends would also help.

But the campaign took an unforeseen turn. Conservative Texas Democrats persuaded Lloyd Bentsen, a former Congressman and successful businessman, to enter the race. To Bush's amazement, Bentsen beat Yarborough in the Democratic primary. Now it would be Bush versus Bentsen for the Senate seat.

The Bush campaign was geared up to take on a liberal. Conservative Bentsen, whose views were much the same as George's on many issues, frustrated Bush and his supporters. Although Nixon and his Vice President, Spiro T. Agnew, traveled to Texas to campaign on Bush's behalf,

Bush shows a victory sign before he and his wife voted in 1970.
(Wide World)

and the White House pumped more than $100,000 from a secret fund into the campaign, it was not enough.

Bush had thought a million votes would be sufficient to win, and he received more than a million—1,033,243, to be exact. But Bentsen beat him by more than 200,000 votes.

It was a very painful loss. Getting beat "sent me to the depths," Bush wrote in a note to a personal friend. And his oldest son, George, once told the Washington *Post* that he had never seen his father as far down as he was after his defeat in 1970.

Jim Baker and Bush have been friends since the 1960s. In 1988 Bush named Baker to be Secretary of State. (The White House)

CHAPTER EIGHT
LOYAL SOLDIER

After his election defeat in 1970, Bush gloomily returned to Washington to serve out the remaining weeks of his term as a member of the House of Representatives. It was a time of reflection. Bush was 46 now, with five children. He knew he wanted to remain in public life, but his career as an elected official had just suffered a hard blow. The future was uncertain.

Meanwhile, at the White House, Bush had not been forgotten. President Nixon told his top advisers that George Bush had talent, money, and the background and desire to do well in public life. Something should be done to help him along, said the President.

Not long after, the telephone rang in Bush's congressional office. It was H.R. Haldeman, the President's chief of staff, a man who held enormous power in the Nixon White House. "When he talked," Bush once noted, "you knew you were listening to the President." Nixon was looking for someone to take over as United States Ambassador to the United Nations, Haldeman said. He wanted Bush to come to the White House and discuss the job.

The idea of being the Permanent Representative of the United States to the U.N. had great appeal to Bush. When the job was formally offered to him, he took it.

Although Bush had no experience as a diplomat and had never gotten very much involved in foreign policy matters as a member of Congress, he earned high marks for his work at the U.N. He listened; he learned. He built personal friendships with his fellow delegates.

But overall, the experience was very painful for him. The biggest and toughest issue facing the United States in the U.N. at the time concerned the People's Republic

Bush, as Texas congressman, poses with President Nixon, who played a vital role in Bush's career. (National Archives and Records Administration)

of China, a nation that had been proclaimed in 1949. The People's Republic, once a staunch ally of the Soviet Union, whose armies U.S. soldiers faced during the Korean War, was seeking membership in the U.N.

At first American policy was opposed to admitting the People's Republic. Instead, the United States supported the "other" China, the Republic of China, a nation also known as Taiwan, after the island off the southeast China coast where the government was based. Traditionally the government of Taiwan represented the people of China in the U.N.

As international support for the People's Republic built, the United States adopted a "two China" policy—the Unit-

In 1971 Nixon appointed Bush to be U.S. ambassador to the United Nations, succeeding Charles Yost (right). (National Archives and Records Administration)

ed States would support the admission of the People's Republic but only on the condition that Taiwan be permitted to remain as a U.N. member.

It was this policy that Bush sought to advance at the U.N. Meanwhile, secret negotiations were being conducted with the People's Republic by Henry Kissinger, President Nixon's National Security Adviser, and Secretary of State William Rogers. Bush was never told of them, however. He continued to speak out enthusiastically on behalf of Taiwan, not knowing he was pursuing a lost cause.

On October 25, 1971, a crucial vote was taken. U.N. members recognized the People's Republic of China as the official representative of the Chinese people. The Taiwan government was tossed out.

Bush was crushed. He believed that he had blown it. Only much later did he learn that Nixon, Kissinger, and Rogers had never expected him to win.

Garry Wills, writing for *Time* magazine, once asked Bush whether he felt betrayed by his superiors. "No, I didn't feel betrayed," said Bush, "I would have liked to have known what was going on...but not betrayed—that's too strong a word."

In November 1972 Richard Nixon was reelected, scoring a landslide victory over George McGovern. In the months that followed his victory, the President began reshuffling people who made up the executive branch of government.

One day Nixon asked Bush to meet with him at Camp David, the presidential retreat in the Catoctin Mountains

Bush, as U.S. ambassador to the U.N., signals his vote during a U.N. session in New York in 1972.
(Wide World)

of Maryland about seventy miles from the White House. "This is an important time for the Republican party," Nixon told George. "The place I really need you is over at the National Committee, running things."

This offer to become Chairman of the Republican National Committee was a disappointment to Bush. He was hoping the President had more lofty things in mind for him. But Nixon told Bush that he could continue to attend Cabinet meetings and that he would get an office in the Executive Office Building, right across the street from the West Wing of the White House. Nixon himself had a hideaway there. Bush took the job.

What Bush was taking on, without realizing it, was the defense of the Republican Party during some of its most dismal days. Only a few months after Bush accepted the post, the Watergate scandal broke.

The Watergate scandal took its name from the Watergate complex of apartment buildings and offices about ten blocks west of the White House. On June 17, 1972, Washington police arrested five men for breaking into the Democratic party's national headquarters there.

The men were linked to the Committee for the Reelection of the President. They were indicted for a number of crimes, including burglary and wiretapping. Two other aides with ties to the White House were also indicted. Five of these seven men pleaded guilty; the other two were found guilty by a jury.

Early in 1973, as Bush was assuming command at the Republican National Committee, evidence was uncovered that established a connection between the break-in at

Watergate and top White House aides. There was also reason to believe that members of the Nixon administration had attempted to conceal evidence.

President Nixon said he had no part in the planning of the break-in or in attempting to cover it up. Bush believed him. He defended Nixon at every turn, blaming everything on the Democrats and the press.

The situation continued getting worse. Early in 1974 high officials of the Nixon administration—Chief of Staff Haldeman, Domestic Council Chief John Ehrlichman, and Attorney General John Mitchell among them—were indicted for conspiracy, obstruction of justice, and perjury.

Bush, as chairman of the Republican National Committee, addresses the Committee in Washington in 1973. (Wide World)

Each of them was convicted and sentenced to prison.

Next, the House Judiciary Committee recommended that President Nixon be impeached, that is, be made to face charges that he had abused the powers of the presidency and withheld evidence from the committee investigating Watergate. The nation was in shock.

Bush remained loyal to Nixon until August 5, 1974. That day taped conversations were released that disclosed that Nixon had ordered a cover-up as early as June 1972.

Two days later Bush had a letter delivered to Nixon. "It is my considered judgment that you should now resign," the letter declared. Republican leaders called upon the President that same afternoon and also urged him to resign for the good of his party and the country.

When Nixon did resign, on August 9, 1974, Bush heaved a sigh of relief. A great burden had been lifted from his shoulders. But he also felt sad for the President and his family. What had happened was "not merely a political disaster," said Bush, "but a human tragedy."

With Nixon's resignation, Vice President Gerald Ford advanced to the presidency. That left the job of Vice President vacant. It was up to Ford to appoint his successor.

Bush hoped that President Ford would give him the job as a reward for his faithful service during the dark days of Watergate. Bush's chances seemed bright. An informal poll conducted by Ford among Republicans in Congress, in his Cabinet, and in the White House showed that Bush was heavily favored for the post. Of those who responded, 255 favored Bush; 181 picked Nelson Rockefeller, governor of New York, and a leading figure in the Republican party.

Bush was vacationing in Kennebunkport when Ford called him to say he was naming Rockefeller as Vice President. Later, when a Portland television reporter interviewed Bush about Ford's choice, he observed that Bush didn't look upset. "You can't see what I'm feeling inside," said Bush.

Why didn't Ford pick Bush to be his Vice President? According to *Newsweek* magazine, Bush may have been hurt by the fact that his 1970 campaign for the Senate had received $100,000 from a secret White House fund. Part of that money, the article in *Newsweek* said, may not have been properly reported under election laws.

The Ford White House was afraid picking Bush as Vice President might reopen the Watergate mess. No one wanted to take a chance on anything like that happening.

Ford invited Bush to the White House to discuss his future, which once again seemed unsettled. Bush wanted a job that would take him as far as possible from the horrors of the immediate past. Serving as Republican National Chairman during the final months of the Nixon administration had been a nightmare for him. He wanted to get away from Washington for a while; he asked to be chief of the United States Liaison Office in the People's Republic of China. Ford was surprised at the request, but granted it.

The Bushes arrived in Beijing in October 1974. They brought with them their cocker spaniel, C. Fred (named after C. Fred Chambers, a Texas friend of the Bushes'). They did not know until they arrived that dogs were a rarity in China. The People's Republic began exterminating dogs in the 1940s to check the spread of disease. When the Bushes took C. Fred out for a walk, many of the Chinese did not know what to make of him. Some pointed to him and exclaimed, "Mao!" the Chinese word for cat. Others were terrified. Barbara had to keep telling people, "He's only a little dog and doesn't bite."

At the time, there were no formal diplomatic relations between the People's Republic and the United States. As envoy, Bush was to serve as an observer and a point of contact on the diplomatic scene. Although he was in charge of a 266-person mission, his contacts with Chinese diplomats were limited.

To get around, Bush was provided with a Chrysler sedan. But he and Barbara decided they would do much of their traveling the same way the Chinese did—by bicycle.

During the summer of 1975 four of the five Bush children visited their parents in China. Son Jeb and his wife, Columba, remained in Houston, where they lived.

According to son Marvin, who was 19 that summer, being in China made his father feel lucky to be an American. "He looked around and saw people who had none of the basic freedoms that we had taken for granted," Marvin said in an interview with author Dian Dincin Buchman in 1989. "He really felt closer to the United States than at any other period in his life.

"Some people have asked my dad, 'When did you first realize that you wanted to be President of the United States?' A great deal of thinking about it occurred while he was in Peking."

The Bushes remained in China until December 1975,

when George was called home in response to what he termed a "real shocker"—a request from the President to replace William Colby as head of the Central Intelligence Agency, the CIA.

Bush knew that there could be no refusing a request that came from the President himself. He and Barbara started making preparations to return to Washington immediately.

Bush's appointment to be CIA director was confirmed by the Senate in January 1976. But in order to win Senate confirmation, President Ford had to show that Bush was "above politics" by promising that he would not make the new director his vice presidential running mate in November that year.

This turn of events did not make Bush happy. For the second time in sixteen months, he was being denied a chance to seek an office he wanted very much.

Taking over as Director of the CIA was a tremendous challenge for Bush. The agency was in somewhat the same condition as the Republican National Committee during the Watergate period. Congressional investigating committees had recently reported that the CIA had spied illegally on thousands of Americans who had opposed United States involvement in the Vietnam War. The CIA had opened mail and used other illegal means of obtaining information. Because of the investigations and the pounding the agency was taking in the press, morale among CIA employees was at an all-time low.

Bush moved quickly to remedy the situation. He established his headquarters on the seventh floor of the CIA building in Langley, Virginia, turning his back on an office that he had been offered in the Old Executive Office Building, which was next door to the White House. Bush wanted to demonstrate that he was more interested in running the agency than in playing White House politics.

He did some serious housecleaning, firing some administrators, promoting others. And as his deputy director he chose a well-known and much respected CIA professional.

CIA employees hailed Bush for what he did to restore morale. He was also praised for helping to prepare an executive order that was designed to prevent CIA abuses of power in the future.

During the period Bush headed the CIA, right-wing critics of President Ford complained that the agency was underestimating the military strength of the Soviet Union. To muffle the criticism, Bush appointed a committee of nine individuals outside the government to make a second estimate of Soviet strength based upon the same evidence the CIA had used.

Bush called the committee "Team B." There were charges that Team B was "stacked," that its members were hard-line anti-Soviets.

Team B judged Soviet military strength to be far greater than had been reported by CIA professionals. Those who were critical of Team B called these estimates "alarmist." Nevertheless, Team B's report helped to trigger the enormous United States military expenditures that began in 1976 under President Jimmy Carter and that reached a peak during the Reagan administration.

CIA Director Bush arrives in Plains, Georgia, late in 1976 to brief Jimmy Carter, Democratic candidate for President, on the intelligence matters.
(Wide World)

These had not been easy years for George Bush. He had been shuttled from one job to another, serving, as Garry Wills was to put it in *Time* magazine, as "a one-man clean-up squad for the Republicans, the nicest man to send into the nastiest situations."

Bush had wanted to be named Vice President in 1974, following Nixon's resignation. But President Ford picked Nelson Rockefeller. Then Bush wanted to be the vice presidential candidate in 1976. But Republican Senator Robert Dole was the choice.

Bush never complained in public or let his disappointment show. He was always the loyal soldier.

Something new was occupying his mind. When Bush began looking over the field of presidential candidates that had been mentioned for 1980, he failed to see anyone whose qualifications were better than his. He believed that all of the experience he had accumulated over the past ten years—as U.S. ambassador to the U.N., chairman of the Republican party, U.S. liaison in China, then director of the CIA—justified his running for the White House.

He also had become convinced that neither President Jimmy Carter nor the Democratic party was going to be able to solve the problems the nation would face during the 1980s. New blood was needed in the White House.

More than three years before the nominating convention was to be held, Bush spoke to his wife and children about his thoughts. "What would it be like to have a dad as President?" he asked his children. They liked the idea. "If anyone had said something [against his running]," said son Marvin, "I think he would have backed out."

In 1978 Bush began working to achieve his goal. He traveled more than 96,000 miles in 42 states, meeting local Republican officials and explaining what he hoped to do.

He began lining up his team, naming Jim Baker as his chief strategist. He even got a campaign slogan ready: "A president you won't have to train."

CHAPTER NINE

THE CANDIDATE

G eorge Bush announced his candidacy for the Republican presidential nomination in May 1979. A few years earlier, even a few months earlier, the idea of the people of the United States voting for a former director of the Central Intelligence Agency as President would have been unthinkable.

A spy in the White House? It would have been out of the question.

But by 1980, being linked to the CIA was no longer a drawback.

Two events occurred late in 1979 that changed the public's attitude. In November 1979 Iranian students stormed the American embassy in Teheran and took hostage some ninety men and women, including sixty-six Americans (of whom thirteen were released almost immediately). The students demanded the return of the former Iranian leader Shah Mohammed Reza Pahlavi, for trial. The

Bush gets applause from his wife and family members as he announces his candidacy for the presidency at the National Press Club in Washington in May 1979. (Wide World)

Shah was undergoing medical treatment at a hospital in New York.

To get back the hostages, President Jimmy Carter tried diplomatic pressure and even a military rescue mission. Neither worked.

In December 1979 a second event occurred that helped to cast Bush's role as CIA director in a different light. The Soviet Union invaded Afghanistan, their aim being to install a more pro-Soviet leader there.

Bush benefited from these happenings. "I see the world as it really is," he told his audiences, "not as I wish it were....For one fascinating year, I had the job of preparing the national intelligence estimates for the President. I had to tell him what the Russians were up to, and believe me, from that experience I have no illusions about Soviet intentions.

"You've got to be realistic about the Soviets," Bush declared. "And you can't help but be realistic about them once you've been head of the CIA."

At the campaign's start Bush and the other candidates focused on Iowa, New Hampshire, and the other states that held early caucuses—meetings of party members —and primaries. Iowa, as the campaign's first major test, was especially important.

Bush started early in Iowa, quickly winning over the state's important party regulars and building a broad-based organization in the state. He worked Iowa county-by-county, often alone, going into people's homes and talking about himself and the presidency. "The other candidates were there," said one of Bush's aides, "but we were

the only ones out there hustling, hustling to ladies' auc-
tions and chicken barbecues."

Bush's wife and other members of the family worked
in Iowa, too. Son Marvin, 22, a student at the University
of Virginia, took time off from school, and moved to Iowa.
He toured the countryside in a van with Iowa license
plates that read: BUSH 80.

Such hard work is necessary because of the nature of
presidential politics. The people who actually turn out
and vote in the caucuses and primaries want to see the
candidates face-to-face, want to discuss issues with them.
Television advertising can work, of course, but to be really effective it requires advance work on a people-to-people
basis.

Bush was often said to be running the kind of campaign that had carried Jimmy Carter to the White House
four years before. Carter had used winning efforts in Iowa
and New Hampshire as a springboard for victories in other
primaries.

But Bush's situation was much different from Carter's.
When Carter ran, he had no clearcut opponent. Bush did.
He was opposed by Ronald Reagan, who had been established as a heavy favorite. The former movie actor and
governor of California had campaigned for the Republican nomination in 1976, losing by a close decision to
Gerald Ford (who, in turn, lost to Jimmy Carter in the
run for the presidency). Many people who had voted for
Reagan in 1976 were anxious to support him again.

But even without such support, Reagan was a tough
opponent. He spoke firmly on the issues. And with his

warm smile and easy, natural manner, he was extremely effective before live audiences and on television. He was considered a shoo-in for the Republican nomination.

But while Bush sweated in Iowa, Reagan took it easy. The hard work paid off. In what was the most heavily attended series of Republican caucuses in Iowa history, Bush was the clear winner, capturing 31.5 percent of the vote.

The results:

George Bush	31.5%
Ronald Reagan	29.4%
Howard Baker	15.7%
John Connally	9.3%
Philip Crane	6.7%
John Anderson	4.3%
Robert Dole	1.5%
(Undecided)	1.7%

BUSH BREAKS OUT OF THE PACK, blared a headline in *Newsweek* magazine. Indeed, it was true. The victory in Iowa thrust Bush into the ranks of what he liked to call "the bigger shots."

Reagan was the big loser. No longer could he be considered the favorite. People were saying that Bush was on his way to achieving what Jimmy Carter had achieved in 1976, and, of course, Carter had sped all the way to the Oval Office. Bush did nothing to discourage that kind of thinking. "We're going all the way to the White House," George told his followers.

Many observers say the 1980 campaign for the Republican presidential nomination was decided by a debate that took place shortly after the Iowa caucuses, on February 23 at the Nashua High School in Nashua, New Hampshire. It has since come to be known as the "ambush at Nashua." And George Bush was the man who was ambushed. He never recovered.

The Nashua debate was the idea of the Reagan forces. They believed the way to puncture the Bush balloon was to put him up against Reagan one-on-one.

When the idea of a two-candidate debate was proposed to Bush, he liked it. He realized it would show voters that the race was now a two-man contest between himself and Reagan.

Hugh Gregg, who was Bush's campaign manager in New Hampshire, took the debate idea to the publisher of the local newspaper, the Nashua *Telegraph*. The newspaper agreed to sponsor it.

Then the Federal Elections Commission, sort of the governing body of political campaigning, declared that a newspaper couldn't sponsor a two-person debate. All of the other candidates—Bob Dole, Howard Baker, John Connally, John Anderson, and Phil Crane—would have to be invited.

That is just what Bush and Reagan did not want. So the Reagan forces suggested that Reagan and Bush split the debate cost. By so doing, they would be able to leave out the other candidates. But Bush's campaign manager refused to share the costs. Whereupon Reagan agreed to pay the debate's entire cost.

The Bush forces had made a serious blunder. Their decision not to share the costs gave Reagan control of the event.

The afternoon before the debate was to take place, Bush began hearing rumors that the Reagan forces had been calling the other candidates, inviting them to come to Nashua with the idea that they might be given a chance to participate in the debate. Indeed, the rumors were true. Reagan's supporters were beginning to believe that victory in New Hampshire was within their grasp. They felt it was no longer necessary to meet Bush head-to-head. So they decided to extend invitations to the other candidates.

At the high school that night, the fireworks began early. John Sears, who was managing Reagan's campaign at the time, told Bush that Reagan wanted to open up the debate to the other candidates. Bush and his advisers said they didn't think much of that idea. Bush pointed out that the *Telegraph* had established the ground rules for the debate, and it didn't seem proper that Reagan should be trying to change them.

The matter still hadn't been decided when the candidates, along with Jon Breen, the editor of the *Telegraph*, who was to moderate the debate, walked out onto the stage. Breen went first, then Bush, then Reagan, followed by Dole, Baker, Anderson, and Crane. Another appearance that night prevented Connally from attending.

Bush had no wish to compromise. He stared straight ahead, appearing grim and resolute. The Manchester (New Hampshire) *Union Leader* was to describe him as looking "like a small boy who had been dropped off at the wrong birthday party."

The audience was boiling. It was clear that just about everyone wanted to let the other candidates participate. "Get them chairs!" some people shouted.

But Jon Breen was firm. His paper had scheduled a two-candidate debate, he explained, and he would not be pressured into opening it to the others.

Then Reagan took the microphone and began to explain why he wanted the other candidates to participate. Suddenly Breen's voice rang out. "Turn off Mr. Reagan's microphone," he shouted, trying to get control of the proceedings.

Perhaps Breen had forgotten that the Reagan forces had agreed to underwrite the cost of the debate. Reagan had not. "I paid for this microphone, Mr. Green," Reagan said firmly. The crowd roared its approval. (It didn't matter that Reagan had got the moderator's name wrong.)

After that it was straight downhill for George Bush. After the other candidates had left the stage, Reagan routed Bush in the debate, and a few days later, whipped him soundly in the voting. Reagan captured 50 percent of the New Hampshire primary vote. Bush managed to get only 23 percent.

Bush himself, along with every political observer, realized that he had made a whopper of a mistake in New Hampshire. It was not because of anything he said or did. It was because of what he didn't say or do. The public thought he was being unfair when he would not agree to include the other candidates. Once Reagan had said it was all right for them to participate, Bush should have gone along. If Reagan had not seized the microphone in the debate in Nashua, would the primary results in New Hampshire have been any different? It's hard to say. Reagan was more of a hero to New Hampshire Republicans than Bush, and he had been for years. He stood with them on all the important issues of the day. About the only doubts they had about him concerned his age—69—and his vitality, but Reagan campaigned so vigorously in New Hampshire that people forgot how old he was. The debate and its outcome made it even easier to vote for him.

The "ambush in Nashua" wasn't the campaign's only low point. Another took place that summer when Bush was campaigning in Pennsylvania.

In a speech he delivered, Bush discussed a Reagan economic policy that called for a tax cut to stimulate the economy. "Supply-siders," as supporters of this policy are called, believe that reducing tax revenues makes more money available for economic investment. And as increased amounts of money are invested in the economy, in the construction of new plants, new jobs are created. Tax revenues shoot up as a result. In the simplest terms, supply-siders say, to get higher tax revenues, cut taxes.

There seems to be no logic to the idea, at least on the face of it. Those opposed to the theory say that it's mumbo-jumbo. To Bush, it smacked of voodoo—"voodoo economics," he called it.

Hardly had Bush uttered the phrase, than opponents of Reagan's, seeking to point up the impractical nature of his economic policies, began to use it. And they credited Bush as the source. To this day the phrase continues to be heard—much to Bush's discomfort.

After Bush went down to defeat in New Hampshire, he never regained his momentum. Of the thirty-three primaries in which he and Reagan competed, Bush won only four (Massachusetts, Connecticut, Pennsylvania, and Michigan).

But Bush kept campaigning. He would not quit.

Then, early in May, Bush lost to Reagan in Texas. Losing in his home state stunned Bush.

Shortly after, Bush and his top aides met at Bush's home in Houston. Bush was told the situation was hopeless, that his candidacy had no future. Jim Baker offered evidence showing that Reagan now had enough delegates to win the nomination on the first ballot.

Still, Bush didn't want to give up. "We've got primaries coming up in California, New York, and Ohio," Bush said. "We still have a shot at it."

Baker refused to agree. He went through the arguments again. "Besides," he said, "we're running out of money."

Bush finally came to terms with the idea that he had lost. Sadly, he agreed to shut down the campaign.

When the Republican National Convention opened in Detroit on July 14, 1980, everyone knew the nominee was going to be Ronald Reagan. The primaries had settled that. The only matter to be decided was the identity of the Vice President.

George Bush went to Detroit hoping and believing he

would be Ronald Reagan's choice. Logic was on his side. In all of the polls of convention delegates and party leaders, Bush was the number one choice, and for good reason. He had proved himself to be a tireless and enthusiastic campaigner over the past two years. He had carried the day in the industrial states of the Northeast, where Republican victories would be vital in the presidential race.

Most important, Bush, who had served as United Nations ambassador and chief of the Liaison Office in the People's Republic of China, offered the Republicans top-flight foreign policy experience. Reagan had none.

Nevertheless, Bush felt that Reagan wasn't absolutely convinced that he was the man for the job. And he was realistic enough to realize that party loyalty and previous experience didn't count for a great deal. All that did count was Ronald Reagan's opinion.

"I don't *really know*," Bush confessed to Michael Kramer of *New York* magazine on the plane flight to Detroit. "I think it'll be me, but I don't have a real feel for it. I'm pretty damn nervous."

Bush had good reason to be nervous. Reagan wasn't convinced that Bush was the man for the job. His doubts about Bush went back to the New Hampshire primary, to the debate in Nashua. Reagan couldn't understand why Bush had sat in his chair that night and not spoken to any of the other candidates when they filed onto the stage. Reagan told an aide he thought that Bush lacked "spunk"—meaning he wasn't bold or aggressive enough.

Other people said that Reagan hesitated about choosing Bush because of Bush's "voodoo economics" remark. When Bush got to Detroit, there was little he could do to boost his own cause. "Our strategy is no strategy," he said. It was all up to Ronald Reagan. Jack Kemp, the congressman from New York, wanted the vice presidential nomination. So did Indiana Senator Richard Lugar.

And then there was former President Gerald Ford. Bush believed that Ford supported him for the vice presidential slot. But when Reagan asked Ford to consider becoming his Vice President, Ford said he'd think about it. He forgot his loyalty to Bush.

Reagan was to have second thoughts about making Ford his Vice President. When Ford finally turned down the offer, the problem was solved. Since Bush was, as Michael Kramer put it, "first choice in the veepstakes," Reagan had no choice but to bow to the will of the party faithful.

Bush was in his suite of rooms at the Pontchartrain Hotel in Detroit when the telephone rang. Jim Baker answered it. Ronald Reagan was calling. Barbara Bush shooed everyone out of the room to give George some privacy. Baker handed Bush the phone. "Hello, George," he heard Reagan say. Then he offered him the vice presidential spot on the ticket. George quickly accepted it.

The next morning the Bushes visited the Reagans for coffee. As they were leaving, Barbara stepped up to Reagan and said, "You're not going to be sorry. We're going to work our tails off for you."

And they did. In fact, both Reagan and Bush campaigned feverishly that summer and fall. Carter, troubled by the hostage problem, campaigned little, leaving it mostly to Walter Mondale, the vice presidential candidate, cabinet members, and his aides.

The Reagan-Bush ticket scored a smashing win. George

Ronald Reagan, George Bush, and their wives, along with former President Gerald Ford and his wife, Betty (left), wave from the podium of the Republican National Convention in 1980.
(The White House)

and Barbara Bush, in the first thirty-five years of their married life, had lived in twenty-seven homes in seventeen cities. The Vice President's home in Washington, D.C., would be their twenty-eighth, and they looked forward to occupying it with great enthusiasm.

CHAPTER TEN

A HEARTBEAT AWAY

I nauguration Day: January 20, 1981. The forecast was for rain but the sun broke through and the temperature was in the mid-fifties, making it one of the warmest inaugural days in American history.

The ceremonies take place on the west front of the Capitol, looking toward the Mall and the Washington Monument. The audience was estimated to be 150,000. Tens of millions watched on television.

As the Marine Corps Band played "Yankee Doodle" and "Battle Hymn of the Republic," the official guests arrived in a solemn line of march to take their positions on the specially constructed podium. Members of the Senate strode in first, then Bush, President Carter, Vice President Mondale, the Justices of the Supreme Court, and then President-elect Reagan.

Custom dictates that the Vice President be sworn into office immediately before the President is inaugurated. The Vice President's oath of office can be administered by the retiring Vice President, by a member of Congress, or some other government official. Bush chose his friend, Supreme Court Justice Potter Stewart.

As Justice Stewart administered the oath, Barbara held the family Bible. Placing his right hand on the Bible, Bush repeated the words in clear and measured tones. Then the Marine Band played a hymn, "Faith of Our Fathers."

Next, Chief Justice Warren Burger administered the oath of office to the new President. As the 21-gun salute

Bush is sworn in as Vice President by Supreme Court Justice Potter Stewart.
(Wide World)

boomed out, Jimmy Carter, a private citizen again, stepped forward and shook Reagan's hand. So began the Reagan era in American history. It was to last eight years. While Reagan was to have a mixed record in handling domestic and foreign issues, and his running of the government was often criticized, he would be praised for the success he and Mikhail Gorbachev achieved in reducing the likelihood of nuclear war.

John Nance Garner, who was Franklin D. Roosevelt's Vice President from 1933 to 1941, is said to have once told fellow Texan Lyndon B. Johnson over the telephone, "Lyndon, the vice presidency ain't worth a pitcher of warm spit."

People have often joked about the office of Vice President, about its lack of responsibility and power. But in the past half century or so, the office has taken on increasing importance.

Beginning in 1933, with the presidency of Franklin D. Roosevelt, Vice Presidents have regularly attended meetings of the President's Cabinet. President Dwight D. Eisenhower included his Vice President, Richard Nixon, not only in Cabinet meetings but in meetings of the National Security Council. (Congress made the Vice President a member of the National Security Council in 1949.) Eisenhower also involved Nixon in the decision-making process at the White House.

President John F. Kennedy also expanded the duties of the Vice President. Kennedy's Vice President, Lyndon B. Johnson, served as chairman of the National Aeronautics and Space Council. Johnson also headed the President's Committee on Equal Employment Opportunity.

Johnson, after he became President, further extended the duties of the Vice President. So did Richard Nixon, who succeeded Johnson in the White House.

When Jimmy Carter took office in 1977, his Vice President, Walter F. Mondale, was one of his most trusted advisers. Carter asked Mondale to help develop U.S. policy on southern Africa. He also assigned the Vice President to help draft a plan to reorganize American intelligence agencies.

So it was with Ronald Reagan and George Bush. While it was Bush's style to keep in the background, Reagan gave him many domestic and foreign assignments that won him public recognition.

Reagan named Bush to head the National Security Council's special situation group or "crisis management team."

He made Bush head of a Presidential task force on regulatory relief, a task force to coordinate federal efforts to assist local authorities in investigating a series of child murders in Atlanta, Georgia, and still another task force to deal with illegal immigration, crime, and drug smuggling in Florida.

Not long after the Inauguration, the Bushes moved into the Vice President's house, a white, four-story Victorian mansion with 33 rooms. Dating back to the nineteenth century, the house is on the grounds of Washington's Naval Observatory, a fifteen minute limousine ride from the White House.

A gatehouse guard checked all visitors' identification before directing them up a winding drive. At a second gate another sentry double-checked credentials, then called the house to announce the visitor's arrival.

The second floor sitting room was one of the coziest rooms in the whole house. There the Bushes often watched the evening news.

In the room was a white telephone that Mrs. Bush never picked up. Anytime President Reagan called the Vice

Bush, as Vice President, conducts a press conference outside the Vice President's home in Washington.
(The White House)

President, the White House operator would first call the Bushes on their regular telephone to tell them a "secure call" was coming. Then the Vice President would go into the sitting room and pick up the white phone.

When the Vice President wanted to call President Reagan, he pressed a signal button on the white phone, and said, "I'd like to talk to the President. Please tell him that in my judgment it's fairly important."

"I don't call him to see how he's feeling," Bush once said.

While the Vice President saw the President frequently and came to be recognized as one of his most loyal advisers, Bush was careful not to be overly friendly with him. He once explained that he called his boss "strictly 'Mr. President.'"

"It has to do with patriotism," Bush said. "With the feeling that goes with the Oval Office. It's part of the presidency."

Life as the Vice President had a frantic quality to it, Bush found. Nevertheless, he and his wife made it a point to have some quiet time whenever possible to enjoy one another's company.

Each morning they awoke at six to the offerings of a Washington country-music station. "We read the newspapers," Barbara once said, "have our juice and coffee in bed, and watch the TV news all at once. That's our hour for communication.

"We're morning people. We wake up feeling good and talk lots. At seven George showers, dresses, and is out."

After his 9 A.M. meeting with the President, the Vice President might read, answer mail, see callers, or have appointments.

The Vice President's only official duty is as presiding officer of the Senate. He has the title "President of the Senate."

As such, he performs the duties of a chairperson, which gives him a special power. A Senator can speak only after being recognized by the Vice President (or, in the Vice President's absence, the president *pro tempore* of the Senate).

The Vice President has the power to make rulings in disputes involving the rules of Senate procedure. But the Senate can reject the Vice President's ruling by a majority vote. The Vice President is also in charge of counting the electoral votes following a presidential election.

The Vice President of the United States, as it is often said, is "only a heartbeat away" from the most powerful elective office in the world. He must be ready to become President at a moment's notice should the President die, resign, or be removed from office.

Eight Vice Presidents have become President because of the death of a President. These "accidental Presidents," as they are sometimes called, were: John Tyler, Millard Fillmore, Andrew Johnson, Chester A. Arthur, Theodore Roosevelt, Calvin Coolidge, Harry S. Truman, and Lyndon B. Johnson.

George Bush, as Vice President, almost became President. The day is etched in his memory.

On Monday morning, March 30, 1981, just seventy days after he had been on the job, Bush boarded *Air Force Two* for what he believed was going to be a routine trip. It called for him to leave Washington early in the morning for Texas, and return that night. There would be two stops, one in Fort Worth, the other in Austin. There would be three speeches, a meeting with Governor Bill Clements, and two press "availabilities," or news conferences.

In detail, the schedule looked like this:

Schedule
THE VICE PRESIDENT'S TRIP TO TEXAS
Monday, March 30, 1981

8:55 A.M., EST	Depart Andrews Air Force Base en route to Fort Worth, Texas
10:45 A.M., CST	Arrive Fort Worth, Carswell Air Force Base
10:50 A.M., CST	Depart Carswell Air Force Base en route to Hyatt Regency Hotel
11:10 A.M., CST	Unveiling of plaque at the Hyatt Regency, formerly Old Hotel Texas
12:00 noon, CST	Address the Texas and Southwestern Cattle Raisers Association; Tarrant County Convention Center
1:20 P.M., CST	Depart Tarrrant County Convention Center en route to Carswell Air Force Base
1:45 P.M.	Depart Carswell Air Force Base en route to Austin, Texas

Traveling with the Vice President were several members of his staff, a number of guests, a dozen or so reporters, and his Secret Service detail. A White House communications specialist, a military aide, and a doctor were also assigned to the trip.

The trip's main event was to be a speech to the Texas State Legislature in Austin. Flying time from Fort Worth to Austin was forty-five minutes.

As *Air Force Two* taxied down the runway at Carswell Air Force Base and lumbered into the air, Ed Pollard, the agent in charge of the Vice President's Secret Service detail, entered Bush's cabin with tragic news. There had been an attempt made on President Reagan's life. The first report said the President was uninjured but that "two agents were down."

"Where did it happen?" Bush wanted to know.

"Outside the Washington Hilton," Pollard said. As he left the cabin, the grim-faced Pollard added, "I'll let you know when we get more information."

The next thing Bush knew the cabin phone was buzzing. Secretary of State Alexander Haig was calling. "There's been an incident," Haig said. "The feeling is that you ought to return to Washington as soon as possible." Haig said a coded message would be teletyped to the plane in a few minutes.

Right after Haig's call, the phone buzzed again. It was Donald Regan. As Secretary of the Treasury, Regan was in charge of Secret Service operations. Regan, like Haig, urged Bush to cut short his trip and return to Washington.

Moments later the teletyped message that Haig had mentioned came through. The early reports had been misleading. The President had been shot and was undergoing emergency surgery at the George Washington University Hospital in Washington.

Air Force Two was approaching Robert Mueller Airport in Austin and preparing to land. As the huge plane touched down and taxied to a stop, Bush, quiet and tight-lipped, scarcely noticed. What if Ronald Reagan should die? The gravity of the situation was beginning to sink in.

Once the plane had landed, Bush called the White House and talked to his chief of staff, Dan Murphy, who offered more details. As Reagan was leaving the Hilton Hotel and about to enter his limousine, a lone gunman had fired six shots at the President and his party. A bullet had entered the President's body under his left arm. Three other people were also wounded—one of the President's Secret Service agents, a Washington police officer, and the President's Press Secretary, James Brady, who was near death.

The President was still in the operating room, Bush was told. There was no word about his condition.

Bush made the decision to head back to Washington at once. But before *Air Force Two* got airborne again, Bush closed himself in the front cabin. He wanted a few moments to collect his thoughts and to say a prayer for Ronald Reagan.

As Bush's plane headed back to Washington, the Vice President spoke by telephone to Attorney General Ed Meese, a close friend of the President's. It was agreed that after *Air Force Two* had landed, Bush would head for the White House to meet with members of Reagan's Cabinet and the National Security Council. This would be a way to show the nations of the world that the United States had not been made powerless, that the wheels of government were still turning.

About half an hour before *Air Force Two* was scheduled to land at Andrews Air Force Base, Ed Meese called with the news that Bush and his staff had been hoping and praying for. The President was out of the operating room. Surgeons had removed the bullet. He was no longer in danger.

As *Air Force Two* roared through the darkening sky, Bush prepared for his meetings at the White House with the Cabinet and the National Security Council. When the meetings were over, it was decided that Bush would go before the White House press corps and answer questions. It would be another way of reassuring the American people that the executive branch of the government was still in full operation.

When Bush returned to Andrews Air Force Base after a day-long trip, it was usual for him to board a marine helicopter and be whisked to the landing pad near the Vice President's residence and then take a car to the White House. The simplest thing to do would be to take a helicopter directly to the White House.

But as *Air Force Two* began its descent into Andrews Air Force Base, Bush had second thoughts about his arrival plans. He knew that television cameras would be waiting at the South Lawn of the White House as the helicopter approached and landed. They'd capture the scene as he stepped out with his aides and hurried into the White House.

The American people would get a message that the Vice President was taking over, Bush believed. That was not the image that Bush wanted to communicate.

Bush called for Lieutenant Colonel John Matheny, his military aide, and told him that he wanted to change his arrival plans. There'd be no helicopter. He'd travel from Andrews Air Force Base by White House limousine.

"But we'll be arriving at rush hour," Matheny said. "The traffic will delay our arrival time at the White House by ten or fifteen minutes."

"Maybe so," said Bush, "but we'll just have to do it that way."

Matheny nodded in agreement. But he looked puzzled.

Bush offered an explanation. "John," he said, "only the President lands on the South Lawn."

For the next two days, Bush pinch-hit for the President. He ran a previously scheduled Cabinet meeting and a session with congressional leaders. He went over political strategy and appointments with the White House staff and heard intelligence briefings. He hosted a luncheon for the prime minister of the Netherlands.

Bush did not move into the Oval Office but continued to use his own office. In the Situation Room, where the Cabinet met, he continued to use his own chair, leaving the President's empty.

"The President is still President," he told the Cabinet. "He is incapacitated and I am not going to be a substitute President. I am here to sit in for him while he recuperates. But he is going to call the shots."

Bush earned warm praise for the job he did filling in for the President. He was neither brash nor timid. He showed strength and cool judgment. He never overstepped. He struck just the right note.

President Reagan is welcomed home to the White House by Barbara Bush following his hospital stay after assassination attempt in 1981.
(Wide World)

CHAPTER ELEVEN

A SECOND TRY

Reagan and Bush developed such an excellent working relationship that no one was surprised when Reagan asked Bush to be his running mate a second time in 1984. That fall they scored a landslide victory over the Democratic ticket of Walter F. Mondale and Geraldine Ferraro. Their 525 electoral votes and more than 54 million popular votes were the biggest totals in election history.

If there was one outstanding characteristic Bush displayed in the eight years he served as Reagan's Vice President, it was his loyalty to the President. There were cases in which Bush spoke out in favor of Reagan's policies even when they did not match his own views. He defended Reagan at every turn, once saying, "I'm for Reagan—blindly."

Bush seldom spoke at Cabinet meetings out of fear that his remarks would be taken as demonstrating that he disagreed with the President.

Bush was so loyal to the President, he was sometimes

ridiculed for it. "One thing about Bush, he's not a yes-man," went a 1984 joke. "If Ronald Reagan says, 'No!' Bush says 'No!' too."

Cartoonist Garry Trudeau made fun of Bush in his comic strip, *Doonesbury,* saying that Bush, when he became Vice President "put his manhood in a blind trust"—put it on the shelf, that is. Columnist George Will called Bush a "lap dog."

Vice President Bush, as President of the Senate, is seated next to House Speaker Thomas P. (Tip) O'Neill during President Reagan's State of the Union address in February 1986. (The White House)

Such criticism was not entirely fair. "The loyal soldier is not the full story of the Bush vice-presidency," wrote David Hoffman in the Washington *Post*. Hoffman called the Bush record "complex." On some big issues, such as arms control, Bush sought to influence the President. On others, the mounting budget deficit, for instance, he did not.

Occasionally Bush would adopt a narrow position, one that reflected his own background. For example, Bush was known to favor tax breaks for the oil industry.

When Bush differed with the President and wanted to let Reagan know it, he would do so privately. Reagan once approved a secret national security order that was meant to curb the activity of foreign spies. In approving the measure, Reagan also gave the go-ahead to a major expansion of lie-detector tests for thousands of government employees. Opposition to the order got very heated. Secretary of State George P. Shultz threatened to resign.

Bush, carrying a copy of the directive, visited Reagan in the Oval Office. The order was a mistake, Bush told the President. Not long after, the order was revised.

Bush had a chance to explain his views to the President on Thursday each week when he and Reagan had lunch together, either in the Oval Office or a small office next to it. When the day was warm and sunny, they sometimes had lunch on the South Lawn terrace.

The lunches were informal and friendly. There were no aides present. They had no points of discussion planned in advance. They talked about important events; they joked about trivial matters.

The President might ask Bush to tell him about the projects on which he was working. If the Vice President had an overseas trip scheduled, the two men might discuss the message that the President wanted Bush to deliver to his foreign hosts.

Some observers say that Bush's greatest influence with the President concerned foreign affairs, particularly in dealing with the Soviet Union. Take what happened in 1983. On September 1 that year, the Soviet Union shot a South Korean airliner out of the sky, killing all 269 people aboard. The attack occurred in Soviet Air Space, and the plane crashed into the Sea of Japan. The Soviet Union charged that the plane, which carried 240 passengers and a crew of 29, had been on a spying mission.

Most nations of the world looked upon the act with horror. Led by President Reagan, they condemned the Soviets.

In the weeks after the tragedy, Bush began to talk to the President about softening his stand toward the Soviets. Reagan's attitude was "to hell with them," according to one of his advisers. But Bush, along with other Reagan advisers, stressed the importance of keeping open the line of communication with the Soviets.

The result was that in January 1984 Reagan delivered a speech in which he reached out to the Soviet Union. It was an address that marked a turning point in Reagan's approach to that nation.

During the years Bush served as Vice President, President Reagan handed him a variety of duties and responsibilities. For instance, in January 1982 the President named Bush to head a cabinet-level task force that was assigned to develop solutions to South Florida's problems with illegal immigration, crime, and drug smuggling.

The task force was successful in developing a cooperative effort between domestic agencies and foreign governments that resulted in the seizure of tons of drugs coming into the United States. Yet the task force failed to bring about any reduction in the amount of drugs available to users for purchase. Indeed, in 1989, the price of illegal cocaine on the streets of New York was substantially lower than it had been in the mid-1980s, reflecting a greater supply. As for South Florida's problems of crime and illegal immigration, solutions were still being sought as the decade drew to an end. On the basis of what it actually achieved, the Bush task force was less than successful.

Bush was also active on the international scene. He journeyed to every corner of the globe, visiting 76 nations. In February 1984 he traveled to London, Rome, and Paris to consult with the leaders of the British, Italian, and French governments. In May that year he made official visits to Japan, Indonesia, Pakistan, and Oman.

In 1985 Bush headed the United States delegation to the funeral of Soviet leader Konstantin Chernenko and met General Secretary Mikhail Gorbachev.

Bush takes pride in some of the duties he carried out as Vice President. There was, for example, a visit to the very troubled Central American country of El Salvador in December 1983.

The government of El Salvador, a country about the size

of the state of Massachusetts, was trying to combat a guer-
rilla movement, which, according to Bush, "was clearly
sponsored by its communist neighbor Nicaragua."

The administration of Ronald Reagan strongly supported the existing Salvadoran government with military aid.
In 1983 that help was being jeopardized by extreme right-
wing death squads operating in El Salvador. Organized
to kill those suspected of supporting the Communists, the
death squads were blamed for over one thousand deaths
in 1983. The U.S. Congress, revolted by what the death

*As Vice President, Bush traveled to every corner of the globe.
Here he is greeted by Egytian president Hosni Mubarak in
Cairo. In background, Suzanne Mubarak kisses Barbara
Bush.*
(Wide World)

squads were doing, had become reluctant to vote additional military aid to El Salvador.

Bush's job was to tell Salvadoran president Alvaro Magaña and other national leaders (including José Napoleon Duarte, the man who would be elected to succeed Magaña) that the activity of the death squads would have to be halted and human rights would have to be respected. Otherwise they could not expect American aid to continue. Bush also had to see to it that his message made an impression upon the generals who ran El Salvador's military.

From the moment *Air Force Two* touched down in El Salvador, Bush knew that his assignment was not going to be any tea party. At the edge of the airfield, he could see men in military garb, guns at the ready, guarding against possible attack.

Bush and his aides were whisked to a building not far from the airport for the first of a series of meetings. Armed soldiers were everywhere. Hours later a formal dinner was held for the American delegation in a room bursting with virtually every important Salvadoran military and political figure.

When it was Bush's turn to offer a toast, he rose and said: "Mr. President, you and many other Salvadorans have demonstrated extraordinary personal courage against tyranny and extremism."

Then came the important part, "But your cause is being undermined by the murderous violence of reactionary minorities....right wing fanatics.

"Every murderous act they commit poisons the well of friendship between our two countries....These cowardly death-squad terrorists are just as repugnant to me, to President Reagan, to the United States Congress, and to the American people as the terrorists of the Left."

Bush felt his words had impact. The killings abated and, by the end of the decade, remained far below the level of the early 1980s, although El Salvador remained a nation under siege. Bush had clearly and forcefully delivered America's message.

During the years he served as Vice President, an event occurred that guaranteed George Bush a special place in the history books. It happened suddenly, almost without any advance warning.

On Friday, July 12, 1985, President Reagan entered Bethesda (Maryland) Naval Hospital just outside Washington for minor surgery. It involved the removal of a small portion of his colon, a part of the large intestine that leads to the end section, called the rectum.

The surgery was to take from thirty to forty-five minutes. A similar growth had been taken out of the President in 1984.

Dr. Daniel Ruge, the chief White House physician, called the tiny polyp "something you don't have to worry about." No one in Washington was at all fearful.

Bush was in Boston, scheduled to visit an industrial site the next day and speak at a Republican party dinner that night. But he was thinking beyond these commitments to a family vacation in Maine that was to begin the next day. For weeks he and Barbara had looked forward to being reunited with their children and grandchildren.

Then fate took a hand. During the time the polyp was

being removed from the lower portion of the President's colon, the doctors looked further. In the upper portion of Reagan's large intestine, they found another polyp. This growth was larger and had fingerlike projections. It might even be cancerous. Whether it was cancerous or not, it was going to have to be removed, requiring more serious surgery. The surgery was scheduled for the next day.

The news sent shock waves through Washington. Some of Reagan's staff seemed dazed. Others wept at their desks.

Reagan called Bush to tell him what the doctors had found and that he planned to have surgery right away. He also told him that during the time he was undergoing surgery and under anesthesia, and thus unable to carry out his duties, he was considering transferring the powers of the presidency to his Vice President.

Bush was stunned. He told the President he would return to Washington immediately. Reagan advised against this. It would make for a crisis atmosphere, the President said, and he urged Bush to stick to his original plans. Bush agreed.

The next day, shortly before the surgery took place, Reagan met with his advisers. They decided to hand the reins of government over to Bush. A letter was prepared and signed by Reagan. It notified the Speaker of the House, Thomas P. O'Neill, and the president *pro tempore* of the Senate, Strom Thurmond, that the Vice President would assume the duties of the President "commencing with the administration of anesthesia to me." Bush, meanwhile, had changed his mind, and flown back to Washington.

So it was that at 11:28 A.M. on Saturday, July 13, 1985, George Bush became the first man ever formally designated to be acting President of the United States. He held that designation until 7:22 P.M., when Reagan reclaimed the office.

The surgery was successful and Reagan made a quick recovery. Within a few weeks the President's health was no longer a subject of major concern.

The incident marked the first time a President had used the third section of the Twenty-fifth Amendment to the Constitution. That section states that if a President declares himself "unable to discharge the powers and duties of his office," the Vice President takes over until written notice that the President is ready to resume control.

The Twenty-fifth Amendment was ratified in 1967. Reagan's use of it was applauded by the amendment's supporters. "The whole idea was to make the transfer [of power], when necessary, business as usual," said former Senator Birch Bayh, who had been one of the sponsors of the amendment. "This is just the kind of situation we were thinking about."

Not long after Reagan and Bush had been reelected in 1984, Bush began a quite campaign for the 1988 Republican presidential nomination. The first step was a meeting with Lee Atwater, a political consultant from South Carolina. Once described as "a born schemer" by a high school buddy, Atwater had worked on Ronald Reagan's presidential campaigns.

Bush told Atwater two things: he had decided to run for the presidency; he wanted Atwater to manage his campaign.

In the weeks that followed, other individuals were added to the team. They included Robert Teeter, his poll taker; Craig Fuller, his chief of staff, and Nicholas Brady, a close adviser. The inner circle also included Bush's wife, Barbara.

Bush had been a part of every Republican presidential campaign since 1964, except for the 1976 race when he was director of the Central Intelligence Agency. He knew better than anyone else what to do.

He and his team worked like a well-oiled machine. State by state, they put together a campaign organization involving thousands and thousands of individuals. "We were an army of ants," one campaign worker recalls.

On October 13, 1987, when Bush formally announced he was beginning a second quest for the presidency, a number of political observers pointed out that the historical odds were very much against him. It had been more than 150 years since a candidate, while serving as Vice President, had been elected directly to the White House. The previous Vice President whom voters had sent to the nation's highest office was Martin Van Buren, in 1836.

Van Buren, like Bush, had a warm and close relationship with his President, Andrew Jackson. Van Buren, in fact, in his inaugural address in March 1837 declared that he intended to "tread in the footsteps" of Jackson, setting a pattern of loyalty to the President that Bush would follow.

Being a true-blue loyalist both helped and hurt Bush. For example, late in 1987 Ronald Reagan met with Soviet leader Mikhail Gorbachev in Washington. Out of the meetings came a historic nuclear missile treaty. Known as the INF (for Intermediate Nuclear Force) Treaty, it called for the elimination of an entire class of nuclear-armed missiles.

Bush was not a major figure in the treaty negotiations, but he shared the spotlight with Gorbachev on several occasions. He was with the Soviet leader when Gorbachev stopped their limousine in downtown Washington to mingle with Americans in front of reporters and photo-

Bush signs autographs during New Hampshire campaign stop in October 1987.
(Wide World)

graphers. And Bush was again in the news when he saw Gorbachev and his wife off at Andrews Air Force Base.

While his involvement with the summit conference boosted his stature, some people said Bush was damaged by what came to be known as the Iran-contra affair, the worst foreign policy embarrassment of the Reagan years. It involved a secret effort by the Reagan administration to sell missiles and other equipment to "moderate" elements in Iran. The hope was that the sale would help gain the release of seven Americans then held hostage by the Iranian government. President Reagan authorized the sales despite warnings from some of his Cabinet members that it was wrong to do so.

Apparently unknown to the President, the money derived from the sales was to go to the rebel forces— "contras"—in Nicaragua. The contras, strongly supported by members of the President's National Security Council, were battling the Communist-supported Sandinista government. The United States Congress had voted to curtail financial aid to the contras.

The policy of attempting to trade arms for hostages eventually brought shame to the nation. The confusion in establishing and carrying out foreign policy, and the obvious lack of presidential control over staff members and their activities, deeply scarred the Reagan presidency.

At first, Bush said he "supported the President." Later he stated he "expressed misgivings." Still later he said he was "out of the loop," that is, not present at some key meetings.

What was George Bush's role in the Iran-contra tangle?

No one knows. Bush said time and again he would not discuss his private conversations with the President, including what recommendations he had made to Reagan about the proposal to sell arms to the Iranians.

Rivals of Bush's believed that his involvement with the Iran-contra affair would anger the voters and damage his chances for the presidency. But as the primary season and the election itself were to demonstrate, his rivals were wrong.

CHAPTER TWELVE

ELECTION VICTORY

I f there was one thing that hurt Bush in the early stages of the 1988 presidential campaign, it was his image. Most people looked upon him as dependable and honest but not very exciting or inspiring. He was sometimes described as a "wimp," meaning a person who is weak and unable to perform effectively.

"The wimp factor," as it was called, was said to be doing Bush great harm. But amazingly Bush was able to shed his wimp image during the 1988 primary campaign.

Bush had five opponents in the primaries. They included Senator Bob Dole of Kansas, the Republican Senate leader since 1985; New York Representative Jack Kemp; television evangelist Pat Robertson; Reagan's first secretary of state, Alexander Haig, and former Delaware governor Pierre S. du Pont.

As the campaign got underway, the Bush forces were worried. The first political contest of 1988 was the Iowa caucuses, meetings of party members in which they would name the candidates they favored. Polls taken in Iowa showed that Bush was in trouble, trailing Bob Dole by a big margin.

And the polls proved to be right. Bob Dole won the Iowa caucuses. Pat Robertson finished second. Bush was jolted by a third place finish. It was embarrassing.

The New Hampshire primary was scheduled the very next week. Bush and his advisers knew he needed a victory there to keep the campaign alive.

At seven o'clock in the morning after his defeat in Iowa, Bush, in a terry-cloth bathrobe, met with the key members of his campaign staff in his hotel suite in Manchester, New Hampshire. "We can't waste any time pointing fingers at each other," Bush said. "This is nobody's fault. We're here in New Hampshire, and all I want to do is everything we can do to win this."

New plans were drawn up, new strategies were mapped out. Bush tried a more man-of-the-people campaign style. He toured shopping malls and factories. He dined at truck stops and McDonald's. He posed in forklifts and at a dog sled race.

Peggy Noonan, one of Reagan's favorite speechwriters, was brought in to give Bush's words a more human tone.

New Hampshire Governor John Sununu (who later would be named chief of staff at the Bush White House) headed campaign operations in the Granite State. It was Sununu who told Bush to get out of his limousine and into a pickup. He told him to get out and shake hands. Sununu also supervised the placing of thousands of phone calls to party faithful, urging them to vote on primary day.

Television was a key element, of course. The Bush team devised a commercial that attacked Dole as "Senator Straddle," unable to make his mind up on the various issues.

At first, Bush didn't want to use the commercial, thinking it was too critical of a fellow Republican. Sununu and the others tried to convince him to go ahead with it. "I don't see anything wrong with it," said Barbara Bush. The commercial was approved. Bush bounced back in New Hampshire, defeating Dole and regaining his status as the man to beat.

Less than three weeks later Bush scored an even greater victory. It was Super Tuesday, when voters in sixteen states went to the polls. Bush swept those sixteen primaries, losing only to Pat Robertson in the Washington state caucuses. Bush won more delegates on Super Tuesday— 574—than any other Republican candidate has ever won in a single day.

Pat Robertson's campaign all but collapsed following Super Tuesday. Soon after, Jack Kemp quit. Haig and du Pont had withdrawn earlier. Dole's campaign limped along for another three weeks, then he too dropped out of the race.

Bush clinched the nomination on Tuesday, April 26, with an overwhelming victory in the Pennsylvania primary. According to a tally in the New York *Times*, that victory brought his nationwide total of delegates to 1,139, a majority of the 2,277 delegates who would be attending the convention.

Bush's clinching of the nomination came less than three months after his disastrous third-place finish in the Iowa caucuses. "Probably the best thing that happened to me," Bush said, "was getting my brains beaten out in Iowa." After Iowa Bush did not lose a single contest of any significance. As for the wimp factor, as the campaign heated up and one primary victory piled on top of another, it simply melted away.

Bush and his wife wave to supporters following Bush's victory in the New Hampshire primary in 1988.
(Wide World)

When the Republican National Convention convened in the Louisiana Superdome in New Orleans in the summer of 1988, Bush's name was the only one placed before the delegates. In a stirring acceptance speech, Bush portrayed himself as both an heir to Ronald Reagan and as his own man, ready to take his seat at the desk in the Oval Office.

"This election—what it all comes down to after all the shouting and cheers," said Bush, "is the man at the desk.

"And who should sit at the desk? My friends, I am that man."

Bush also revealed a glimpse of himself as a private man. "I may sometimes be a little awkward," he said, "but there's nothing self-conscious in my love of country. I am a quiet man, but I hear the quiet people others don't—the ones who raise the family, pay the taxes, meet the mortgage. I hear them and I am moved, and their concerns are mine."

But Bush's moment of triumph at the convention was spoiled by a war of words that broke out over his surprise choice of 41-year-old Senator J. Danforth (Dan) Quayle of Indiana to be his vice presidential running mate. The debate was triggered by the fact that Quayle had joined the National Guard at the height of the Vietnam War, avoiding the risk of being drafted. This eliminated any chance that Quayle might experience combat duty. Quayle spent the years of the Vietnam War going to law school and holding down a series of political jobs arranged by friends of the family.

But the controversy over the boyish-faced Quayle quickly went beyond his service in the National Guard. Serious questions began to be raised about Quayle's qualifications for the number-two job. After twelve years in Congress—two terms in the House of Representatives and almost eight years in the Senate—Quayle was just beginning to make his mark as a legislator. He had not been a leading figure or spokesman on any major issue. Surely there were others better qualified to be a "heartbeat away" from the presidency.

Bush's children, all delegates to the Republican National Convention in New Orleans in 1988, are interviewed by Jane Pauley of NBC-TV (left). They are (from left), George, Jr., from Texas; Neil, from Colorado; John, from Florida; Marvin, from Virginia; and Dorothy Bush LeBlond, from Maine. (Wide World)

During his two terms in the House, Quayle's attendance at floor votes and committee meetings was the worst in the Indiana delegation. In the Senate he was more involved and got higher marks for hard work. His major achievement was to cosponsor, with Democratic Senator Edward M. Kennedy of Massachusetts, the 1982 Job Training Partnership Act.

As heir to a multimillion-dollar publishing fortune, Quayle, as a young man, constantly benefited from his privileged background. Doors were opened for him that might have stayed closed for others. This made Quayle a target for Democratic populists.

Though known to be serious and thoughtful as a Senator, Quayle was vastly overshadowed by many of his colleagues in the Senate. In terms of national reputation, he was on a low rung of the ladder.

Bush explained he had picked Quayle because he was seeking to appeal to a younger generation of voters. "He's different from me," said Bush. "I'm 64 and he's 41, and that's good."

For a time, the Quayle decision seemed as if it might backfire, causing Bush serious harm. At the very least, it got the campaign off to a rocky start. Bush was never able to escape the fact that the idea of a President Quayle made voters very nervous.

As the furor over Quayle was reaching a peak, Jim Baker was taking over as Bush's campaign manager from Lee Atwater. Baker had been occupied as Ronald Reagan's Secretary of the Treasury and, earlier, as his chief of staff. A longtime friend of Bush's, the smooth-operating Baker had directed Bush's first try for the presidency in 1980.

As his Democratic opponent, Bush faced 54-year-old Michael Dukakis, then in his third term as governor of Massachusetts. The son of immigrant Greek parents, Dukakis had cultivated the image of a hard-working, no-nonsense politician. But some observers wondered

The Bushes with vice presidential candidate Dan Quayle and Quayle's wife, Marilyn.
(The White House)

whether this approach made him too impersonal, too insensitive.

Dukakis picked Senator Lloyd Bentsen of Texas as his running mate. Bentsen, who had defeated Bush in the 1970 Senate race, besides running as a vice presidential candidate was also seeking reelection to the Senate. (A dual race is permitted by Texas law.) Bentsen had previously been reelected in 1982.

Bush and his campaign staff devised a simple strategy. They would paint Dukakis as a big-spending liberal who would raise taxes. They would charge that he was soft on crime and weak on defense issues.

Bush went on the attack early, even before Dukakis had been endorsed by the Democratic National Convention, criticizing the Massachusetts governor for vetoing a 1977 bill requiring teachers to lead the Pledge of Allegiance each day. Dukakis and Susan Estrich, his campaign manager at the time, shrugged off the criticism. They did not believe that patriotism could ever become a campaign issue.

It was not until months later that Dukakis finally responded to the attack. He explained that he never opposed recitation of the Pledge, and that he had vetoed the bill because he had received an opinion from the Massachusetts supreme court that the law would be unconstitutional. "If the Vice President is saying that he'd sign an unconstitutional bill," said Dukakis, "then in my judgment he's not fit to hold office."

This incident typified much of the campaign debate. Dukakis was often on the defensive, failing to deliver an overall message to the voters.

"He [Dukakis] entered the campaign a blank slate," said *Time* magazine, " and Bush scrawled all over him." John Sasso, who took over as Dukakis's campaign manager on Labor Day weekend, put it this way: "One of the rules of this business is that somebody gets to fill up the cup. If you want to be successful, you have to fill it up first."

In the same manner, Bush attacked a prison furlough program in Massachusetts. In one case the program had allowed a convicted murderer sentenced to life without parole to escape. The convict later stabbed a man and raped his wife.

A Bush television commercial, meant to show the releasing of dangerous criminals to prey upon the nation, depicted a long line of prisoners shuffling through a revolving door. "America can't afford that!" said a tough-sounding voice.

Again, Dukakis ignored the attack at first. He made no effort to explain the nation's furlough system, its benefits and drawbacks, or compare the various state and federal programs with the one in Massachusetts.

Bush also attacked Dukakis for being a liberal, a "card-carrying member" of the American Civil Liberties Union. This Dukakis reacted to by trying to be deceptive about his background. He ignored the chance to defend liberalism, to stress that protectors of civil liberties can only be applauded.

Dukakis preferred to run what he saw as a positive, issue-oriented campaign. He talked about his "competence" as governor of Massachusetts, and stressed the part he had played in the economic growth of the state. He hit Bush only occasionally. Not until the last two weeks of the cam-

*Governor Michael Dukakis of Massachusetts, Bush's Dem-
ocratic opponent in the 1988 presidential election.*

paign did he begin to deal with the Bush attacks effectively. By that time it was too late.

Another big factor in the election was the second of two debates between the candidates. Bush was relaxed and confident for the second debate. Dukakis appeared dull and uncomfortable. He raised only one of six issues he planned to discuss. Afterward, said *Time* magazine, "he knew he had blown it." The next morning a cartoon in the Boston *Globe* titled "The Third Debate" showed Dukakis sitting in an airplane thinking, "Should I run for reelection as governor?"

Toward the end, President Reagan campaigned vigorously for the Bush-Quayle ticket. One early November swing took him to Missouri, Arkansas, California, Nevada, Wisconsin, and Ohio. At one stop after another, big, enthusiastic crowds turned out as Reagan lashed out at Dukakis on crime, defense, and economic policy.

The campaign's great failing was that the important issues of the day—the nation's budget deficit (estimated to be $150 to $200 billion), defense, and arms control, and such social problems as drugs, homelessness, and the environment—were never really discussed. A vote for Bush was seen by many as a vote for continued peace, prosperity, and high employment.

Bush held a commanding lead in the polls throughout all but the earliest stages of the race. On October 12, almost four full weeks before the election day, Peter Jennings of ABC News announced that according to an ABC News/Washington *Post* poll, Bush had an overwhelming advantage in the battle for the electoral college. Bush was ahead in 21 states with a block of 220 electoral votes, only 50 votes short of the 270 needed to win. Jennings also said that if the fifteen states then leaning toward Bush eventually went his way, he would have an additional 180 electoral votes.

In the final days, as Dukakis fought hard in several key states, he cut into Bush's lead. On the morning of Election Day Bush and his advisers were a bit jittery, as Bush's advantage continued to shrink.

And the first polls of those who had already voted—the "exit polls'—brought more bad news. Bush and Dukakis were running neck and neck in several critical states.

But as the votes rolled in that evening, Bush, watching at his hotel suite in Houston with his wife and several of their children and grandchildren, began to relax. Early returns showed Bush had swept the South and won in Connecticut, Maine, and Missouri.

At 9:17 P.M. Eastern time, CBS News named Bush the winner, followed three minutes later by ABC News. At 10 P.M., President Reagan called to congratulate him. Ten minutes later Dukakis called to concede.

The final results looked like this:

	Popular Vote	Percentage	Electoral Vote
George Bush	48,138,478	53.4	426
Michael Dukakis	41,114,068	45.6	112

Roughly 91 million Americans voted (including those who had voted for candidates representing minority parties). But another 91 million who could have voted didn't. It was the lowest voter turnout for any presidential election since 1924.

In his first weeks in office Bush set out to let the American people know that he was active and involved. President Reagan would sometimes call it a day at 4 or 5 P.M. On Fridays the Reagans usually left very early in the day for the presidential retreat at Camp David, not returning until Sunday.

Bush, by contrast, sought to demonstrate he had much greater enthusiasm for the job. He and Barbara opened the White House for a post-inaugural reception, conduct-

Bush holds up his hands to acknowledge crowd's applause during victory rally in Houston following his win in the 1988 presidential election.
(Wide World)

ing a private tour for the first fifteen of the hundreds of people who waited in line. Bush telephoned nearly two dozen foreign leaders, including Soviet leader Mikhail Gorbachev, to thank them for their congratulatory notes. He met with his political opponents—Michael Dukakis and Lloyd Bentsen, with Jesse Jackson, Pat Robertson, and Bob Dole. He invited several reporters to dinner and

On the morning following the inauguration, the Bushes conducted a private White House tour for these visitors. (The White House; David Valdez)

asked some others to the Oval Office for a question-and-answer session. Bush even went jogging.

In discussing how he would work with Brent Scowcroft, whom he appointed as his National Security Adviser, Bush declared that he meant to be in the thick of foreign policy discussions. "I will take a keen interest in these matters," said Bush, promising he would provide Scowcroft with "direct access day and night."

"I will personally read" the daily intelligence briefing "every morning," Bush added.

Bush also said he wanted to be closely linked to hour-by-hour reports of any world crisis. He was going to be a "shake-me-and-wake-me" President, he said, happy to be roused in the early morning for important news. Ronald Reagan was no "shake-me-and-wake-me" President.

"George Bush is not only going to be the President," said James Cannon, who had served in the White House under President Reagan, "but he is also going to be very different from Ronald Reagan—familiar with details, profoundly engaged with a lot of issues, right in the thick of it all."

Bush moved quickly to build his team. The day after the election, he announced that Nicholas Brady, a close and longtime friend and a former Wall Street investment banker, had agreed to remain as treasury secretary.

Most of the others Bush chose as his cabinet members and those he named to other high level jobs came from an elite group of individuals with long experience in government service. They were often described as Washington "insiders." They included Elizabeth Dole, secretary of labor; Robert A. Mosbacher, secretary of commerce; and James D. Watkins, secretary of energy.

As he took over the reins of the presidency, George Bush could look back on 25 years in public life. He had served in a variety of posts in politics, diplomacy, and intelligence.

Through the years, he had shown himself to be fair and loyal, solid and cautious. He was good at pleasing people.

But as President, Bush was cast in a role new for him. He was no longer a follower, striving to carry out assigned

Bush (center, left) holds first meeting with designated cabinet members.
(Wide World)

tasks or seeking to satisfy the wishes of others. Now Bush was in charge. "He has played in the orchestra," the Washington *Post* noted, "but will he be able to lead it?"

In concrete terms, was George Bush going to be able to persuade a sometimes balky Congress controlled by Democrats to follow his lead? Was he going to be able to stimulate the American people to support his programs? And what about international affairs—was he going to be able to get world leaders to respond to his policies?

George Bush has knowledge and experience in government. He has a practical "can-do" attitude about getting things done. He is eager and enthusiastic. Future events will reveal how well he has mastered the art of leadership.

Important Dates in the Life of George Bush

1924	Born in Milton, Massachusetts, on June 12.
1942	Graduated from Phillips Academy in Andover, Massachusetts on June 4.
1942	Enlisted in the U.S. Navy Reserve as a Seaman Second Class on June 12.
1943	Commissioned as youngest pilot in U.S. Navy. Assigned to U.S.S. *San Jacinto*.
1943—45	Flew torpedo bombers in Pacific theater of operations.
1944	Shot down on September 2 by Japanese fire while on mission in the Pacific.
1945	Married Barbara Pierce of Rye, New York, on January 6.
1946	Birth of eldest son, George Bush, on July 6.
1948	Graduated from Yale with degree in economics.
1948—50	Moved to west Texas; became supply salesman for Dresser Industries.
1949	Birth of first daughter, Robin Bush.

1951	Cofounded Bush-Overby Oil Development Company.
1952	Bush's father, Prescott Bush, elected by Connecticut to U.S. Senate. Served for ten years.
1953	Birth of second son, John (Jeb) Bush, on February 11.
1953	Cofounded Zapata Petroleum Corporation.
1953	Bush's daughter, three-year-old Robin Bush, died of leukemia.
1954	Cofounded Zapata Offshore Company, a firm that pioneered in the construction of offshore drilling platforms.
1955	Birth of third son, Neil Bush, on January 22.
1956	Birth of fourth son, Marvin Bush, on October 22.
1959	Birth of second daughter, Dorothy Bush, on August 18.
1963	Named chairman of Harris County, Texas, Republican organization.
1964	Lost race for U.S. Senate to Democrat Ralph Yarborough.
1966	Elected to the U.S. House of Representatives from the Seventh District of Texas.
1968	Reelected to the U.S. House of Representatives.
1970	Lost race for the U.S. Senate to Democrat Lloyd Bentsen.

1971—73   Served as United States ambassador to the United Nations.

1973—74   Served as chairman of the Republican National Committee.

1974—75   Served as chief of the U.S. Liaison Office in the People's Republic of China in Beijing.

1976—77   Served as director of the Central Intelligence Agency.

1977—80   Campaigned for the Republican presidential nomination.

1980   Named by Ronald Reagan to be his vice presidential running mate in July.

1980   Elected Vice President on November 4.

1981   Sworn in as the Forty-third Vice President of the United States on January 20.

1985   Sworn in to a second term as Vice President on January 20.

1985   Named acting President of the United States for several hours on July 13 in historic transfer of power.

1987   Launched second campaign for the presidency on October 12.

1988   Elected President of the United States on November 8.

1989   Sworn in as the Forty-first President of the United States on January 20.

For Further Reading

Buchman, Dian Dincin. *Our 41st President, George Bush.* New York: Scholastic Books, 1989.

Bush, George, with Gold, Victor. *Looking Forward: An Autobiography.* New York: Doubleday & Co., 1987.

Cannon, Lou. *Reagan.* New York: G.P. Putnam's Sons, 1982.

McTavish, Thistle, and Swenson, Allan. *Bush Country, By George!* Portland, Maine: Guy Gannett Publishing Co., 1981.

Sufrin, Mark. *George Bush: The Forty-first President of the United States.* New York: Delacorte Press, 1989.

Wead, George. *George Bush, Man of Integrity.* Eugene, Oregon: Harvest House Publishers, 1988.

INDEX

About the Author

George Sullivan is a well-known author of books for children and young adults, with more than one hundred titles to his credit. Before becoming a full-time author in the mid-1960s, Mr. Sullivan worked in public relations and in publishing. Before that he served in the navy as a journalist. He grew up in Springfield, Massachusetts, and graduated from Fordham University in New York City.

His many interests are reflected in his writings. Subjects of his popular biographies for young readers have included Mikhail Gorbachev, Egyptian president Anwar Sadat, and Ronald Reagan.